THEMATIC UNIT
ROCKS & SOIL

Written by Janet A. Hale

Illustrated by Sue Fullam and Cheryl Buhler

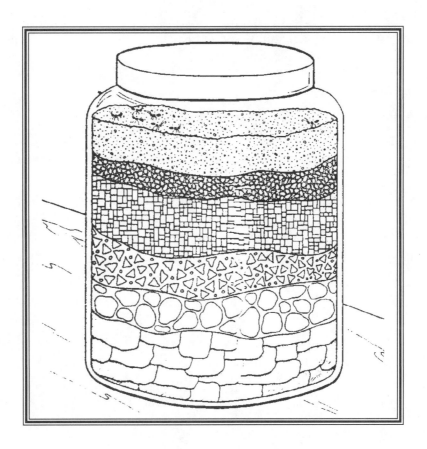

Teacher Created Resources, Inc.
6421 Industry Way
Westminster, CA 92683
www.teachercreated.com

©1992 Teacher Created Resources, Inc.
Reprinted, 2004

Made in U.S.A.

ISBN-1-55734-265-2

Table of Contents

Introduction

Rocks and Soil contains an enjoyable, whole language, thematic unit. Your grade level may require your students to understand rocks and soil. Perhaps your students show an interest in the earth and its structure. For these reasons or others you may have in mind, you will enjoy utilizing this exciting, 80-page, fun-filled, thematic unit which includes reading, language, writing, across the curriculum activities, and homework experiences. The activities incorporate basic skills, critical thinking, and cooperative learning. Share the fun with your students as they become avid rock hounds!

In using whole language/thematic units it is beneficial to build in a day or days that can be used for review time to monitor and adjust student progress. On a daily basis, make mental notes of the skills/concepts students are mastering, as well as areas in which they need practice.

This thematic unit includes:

❑ **literature selections**—summaries of two children's books with related lessons (complete with reproducible pages) that cross the curriculum

❑ **poetry**—suggested selections and lessons enabling students to write and publish their own works

❑ **planning guides**—suggestions for sequencing lessons each day of the unit

❑ **language experience ideas**—daily suggestions as well as activities across the curriculum, including Big Books

❑ **bulletin board ideas**—suggestions and plans for student-created and/or interactive bulletin boards

❑ **homework suggestions**—extending the unit to the child's home

❑ **curriculum connections**—in language arts, math, science, social studies, art, music, and life skills such as cooking

❑ **group projects**—to foster cooperative learning

❑ **a culminating activity**—which requires students to synthesize their learning to produce a product or engage in an activity that can be shared with others

❑ **a bibliography**—suggesting additional literature and nonfiction books on the theme

To keep this valuable resource intact so that it can be used year after year, you may wish to punch holes in the pages and store them in a three-ring binder.

Introduction *(cont.)*

Why Whole Language?

A whole language approach involves children in using all modes of communication: reading, writing, listening, observing, illustrating, experiencing, and doing. Communication skills are interconnected and integrated into lessons that emphasize the whole of language rather than isolating its parts. The lessons revolve around selected literature. Reading is not taught as a separate subject from writing and spelling, for example. A child reads, writes (spelling appropriately for his/her level), speaks, listens, etc. in response to a literature experience introduced by the teacher. In this way, language skills grow naturally, stimulated by involvement and interest in the topic at hand.

Why Thematic Planning?

One very useful tool for implementing an integrated whole language program is thematic planning. By choosing a theme with correlating literature selections for a unit of study, a teacher can plan activities throughout the day that lead to a cohesive, in-depth study of the topic. Students will be practicing and applying their skills in meaningful contexts. Consequently, they will tend to learn and retain more. Both teachers and students will be freed from a day that is broken into unrelated segments of isolated drill and practice.

Why Cooperative Learning?

Besides academic skills and content, students need to learn social skills. No longer can this area of development be taken for granted. Students must learn to work cooperatively in groups in order to function well in modern society. Group activities should be a regular part of school life and teachers should consciously include social objectives as well as academic objectives in their planning. For example, a group working together to write a report may need to select a leader. The teacher should make clear to the students and monitor the qualities of good leader-follower group interaction just as he/she would state and monitor the academic goals of the project.

Why Big Books?

An excellent cooperative, whole language activity is the production of Big Books. Groups of students, or the whole class, can apply their language skills, content knowledge, and creativity to produce a Big Book that can become a part of the classroom library to be read and reread. These books make excellent culminating projects for sharing beyond the classroom with parents, librarians, other classes, etc. Big Books can be produced in many ways and this thematic unit book includes directions for at least one method you may choose.

How to Dig a Hole to the Other Side of the World

By Faith McNulty

Summary

A young boy goes on the adventure of a lifetime by digging a hole through to the other side of the world. During his adventure, your students will learn about the layers of the earth, fossils, oil, volcanoes, the "heat" of the earth, and much more! This story truly embraces the science and literature connection.

The outline below is a suggested plan for using the various activities presented in this unit. You may adapt the ideas to meet needs in your classroom environment.

Sample Plan

Day I

- Read Rock Riddle (#1, page 6)
- The Land That We Love (page 19)
- Discuss "Rock Hound" definition using Bulletin Board Display (page 73)
- Read *How to Dig a Hole to the Other Side of the World*
- Retell story (#2, page 8)
- What An Adventure! (page 40)
- Homework: Cool Tool (page 63)

Day II

- Share Day I homework; display
- Make Earthly Comparisons (page 45)
- Show and discuss "Rock" display (#2, page 6)
- Types of Rocks I (page 20)
- Rock Language (#1, page 7)
- Make Rock Candy (page 61)
- Homework: Rock Hunt (page 63)

Day III

- Share Day II homework; display
- Take a Rock Walk (#2, page 9)
- My Pet Rock (page 49)
- Make Clay Creatures (page 40)
- Reread storybook and retold Big Book version from Day I
- Publish the latest news! "Rock Hound Gazette"(#3, page 10)

Day IV

- Egg-ceptional Earth (page 55)
- A Jar of Topsoil (#4, page 10)
- Discover Mystery Bubbles (#5, page 10)
- Soil Sleep (page 21)
- Discuss Three Kinds of Soil (page 21) or Six Soil Speculations (page 49)
- Sing Soil Song (page 60)
- Enjoy Math Backgrounds (page 46)
- Homework: Mystery Hole (page 63)

Overview of Activities

SETTING THE STAGE

1. Divide the class into pairs. Read the following riddle while displaying a closed lunch bag containing the answer (a rock):

   I can be hot,

   I can be cold.

   Sometimes I'm light,

   Sometimes hard to hold.

   You see me everywhere,

   You use me everyday.

   I help you write,

   work, and play!

   What am I?

   Each team discusses what they predict will be inside the bag. List the predictions. Have students close their eyes and feel inside of the bag without peeking. After everyone has had a chance, ask the total group to tell you what is in the mystery bag. Show the rock. Discuss the meaning of the riddle.

2. Bring in examples of items made from various kinds of rocks and display. Have students try to hypothesize how all of the items are alike. List their ideas. Explain that the items were made from rocks. Take a few minutes to explain how each one is made from a rock. (Some suggestions are: jewelry, potting soil, pencil, chalk, concrete, bricks, coal, a marble dish, salt, the chalkboard.)

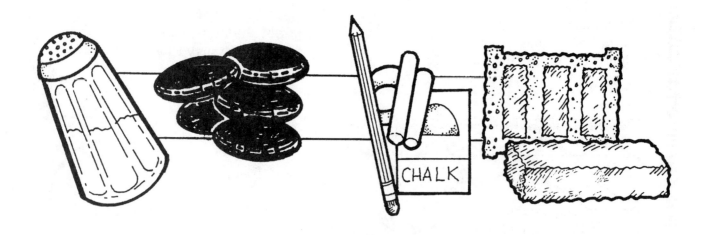

       6

Overview of Activities *(cont.)*

SETTING THE STAGE (cont.)

3. Invite a jeweler to speak to the class about how rocks are turned into gemstones. Ask the jeweler to bring in examples of the gemstones that represent the monthly birthstones. When the guest speaker has finished, students can create their own birthstone rings (pattern, page 11).

   To create the gemstone, cut out a 4" x 4" piece of aluminum foil. Wrap around the cut-out gemstone pattern. Using a permanent marker, student colors with appropriate birthday month's color (see chart below). To create facets, score the colored gemstone with the tip of a blunt pair of scissors. Glue the gemstone to colored ring base. Display or take home.

Month	Birthstone	Color
January	Garnet	Red
February	Amethyst	Purple
March	Aquamarine	Blue or Blue-green
April	Diamond	No color
May	Emerald	Green
June	Pearl	White
July	Ruby	Red
August	Peridot	Green
September	Sapphire	Blue
October	Opal	Rainbow colors
November	Topaz	Yellow or Yellow-brown
December	Turquoise	Blue or Blue-green

ENJOYING THE BOOK

1. For a language experience, have students go outside to find rocks. Explain that they will need to choose rocks by listening for "clue words" in sentences such as: "Find a rock bigger than your fist," "Look for a rock under the ground," or "Show a friend a rock smaller than your thumb." Try to include sentences using the descriptive words: shiny/dull, hard/soft, rough/smooth and big/little (word cards, pages 12–15).

Overview of Activities *(cont.)*

ENJOYING THE BOOK *(cont.)*

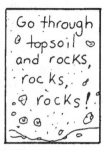

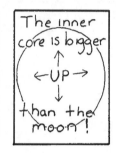

2. Re-create the story text by having the students retell the story. Write their sentences onto paper, changing paper color as the adventure unfolds (see example above). Have students illustrate the pages as teams. Place all the pages together to make a Big Book, or hang pages separately to form a wall story. Read and enjoy the colorful version of today's story!

3. Soil is very important to people, animals, and plants. It is made of minerals, decayed plants, rock particles, water, and air. How much of each of these items are in the soil? Hand out a sheet of paper to each student and have them draw a circle in the center.

Overview of Activities *(cont.)*

ENJOYING THE BOOK *(cont.)*

4. Ask them to divide the paper into sections to show what there is more and/or less of in soil. (Show an example, but not the correct amounts, stressing that fact when modeling.) After they have drawn and labeled their hypothesized circle graphs, draw a large circle on the board and divide it correctly (see below). Discuss the differences.

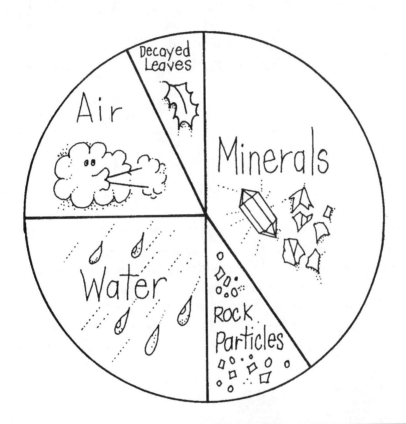

EXTENDING THE BOOK

1. Divide students into teams of two. Show earth's cross-section (see page 16). Review the names of each layer. Provide a large piece of butcher paper and a no-spaceship pattern (Page 17). Teams draw their own cross-section of the earth's layers. Using a black crayon, they are to refer back to the story and draw the path that the no-spaceship took through its adventure. Have each team color and cut out their no-spaceship and place it at their favorite place in the boy's journey through the earth's layers. Display finished projects in the classroom or hallway.

2. Take a walk around school, inside and out. Students observe and inform you of anything and everything they see that is made wholly or partially from rock (even potted plants). After the walk, paint a mural on a long sheet of butcher paper. Label the different things made from rocks. Display in the hallway.

Overview of Activities *(cont.)*

EXTENDING THE BOOK (cont.)

3. Create newspaper articles and illustrations for the Rock Hound Gazette (page 18). Refer students back to the facts in *How to Dig a Hole to the Other Side of the World*, or supply other resource books so students can find the information they will need to write their articles. Collect and compile into a special classroom newspaper and display in the library along with a class rock collection.

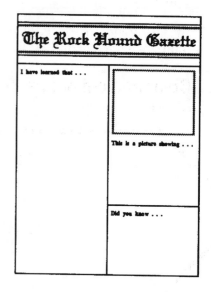

4. **Note:** Prepare for this activity by placing a large, hard rock in the bottom of an empty gallon glass jar. On top of the rock, you will add different types and textures of soil (available at nursery/plant stores) to create a layered effect. Label the jar at the appropriate levels with the words Crust (the rock) and Topsoil (the layers). Explain that what we walk on most of the time is the topsoil of our earth. When we walk on a mountain or a big rock we are actually walking on the earth's crust. Show the prepared jar. Discuss the above concept using the jar as a visual aid. Discuss and leave on display.

5. Mystery Bubbles. Place planting soil loosely inside a large, wide-mouthed jar. Gather students around as you slowly add water to the soil. What do they observe happening? (Bubbles will form.) The bubbles are air that was trapped in the soil coming up to the top. Why is air important to the soil? (Air helps plants breathe.) Air in the soil helps plants, but it also helps animals. On a large sheet of brown butcher paper decorated with a marker to look like underground soil, have students brainstorm all the animals and insects they can think of that live in soil. List and display brainstorming sheet.

10

Gemstone Rings

1. Cut out gemstone. Cover with aluminum foil; color.

2. Score aluminum foil with blunt scissor to make facets.

3. Color and cut out band. Paste gemstone to band.

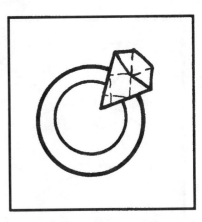

Completed project

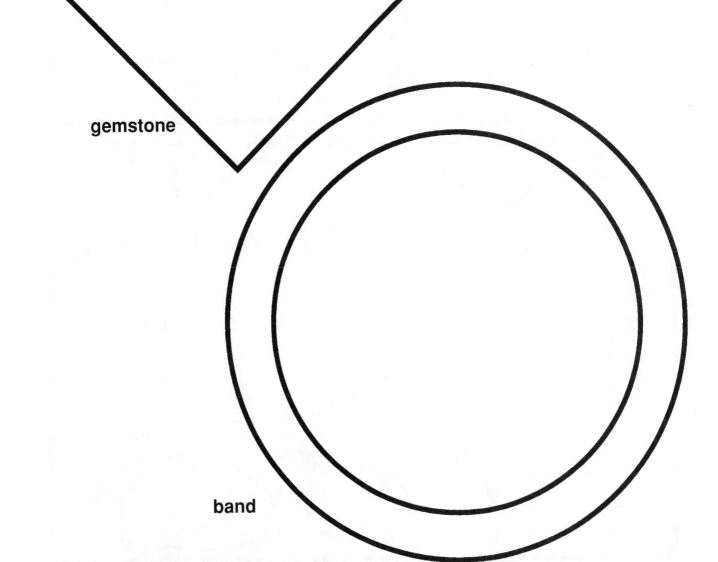

gemstone

band

Rock Description Cards

Rock Description Cards *(cont.)*

Rock Description Cards *(cont.)*

Rock Description Cards *(cont.)*

Inside Our Earth

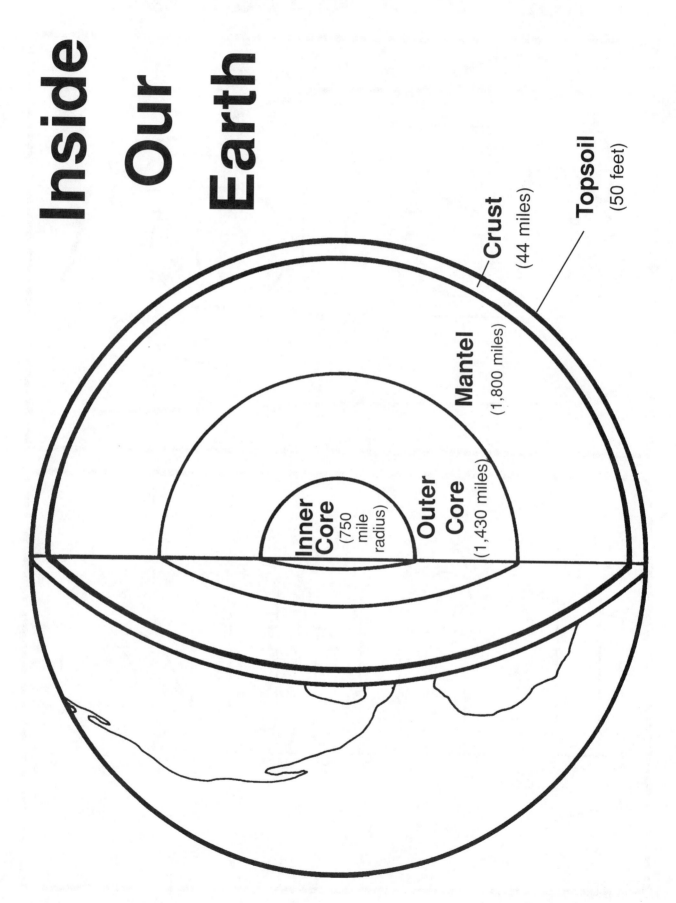

Crust
(44 miles)

Topsoil
(50 feet)

Mantel
(1,800 miles)

Outer
Core
(1,430 miles)

Inner
Core
(750
mile
radius)

No-Spaceship Models

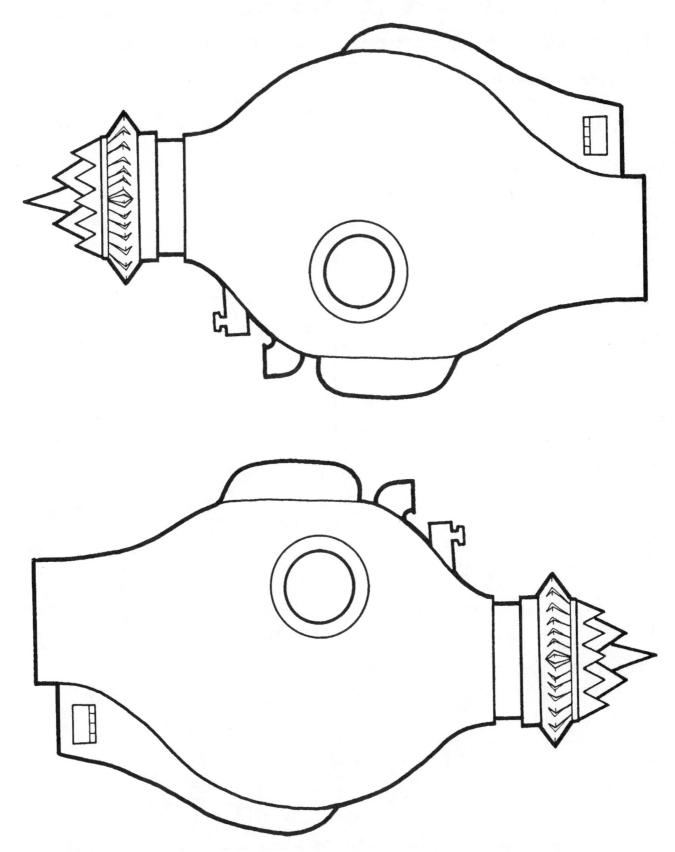

The Rock Hound Gazette

I have learned that...

This is a picture showing...

Did you know...

The Land That We Love

Note: For this activity you will need pieces of construction paper: brown for one-third of your class and blue for two-thirds of your class. The pieces of paper represent the ratio of land (one-third) to water (two-thirds) on the earth's surface.

Begin the activity by having the class observe a globe. What do they see or notice?

Next, hold up a piece of 9" x 12" (23 cm x 30 cm) paper and share the following predictive project with them.

1. Explain that they are to use a blue and brown crayon to illustrate how much of the earth's surface is covered with land and water. They need to pretend that the white paper they will be given is the total earth's surface. After pictures of the earth's surface have been drawn, collect and display on a bulletin board entitled "Land That We Love."

2. Pass out the blue and brown construction paper squares. Students move around the room and classify themselves into land or water. Guide the two groups into a rectangular shape (like the shape of the white paper).

3. Have students compare the results of actual land/water ratio (which they are physically representing) to their hypothesized pictures.

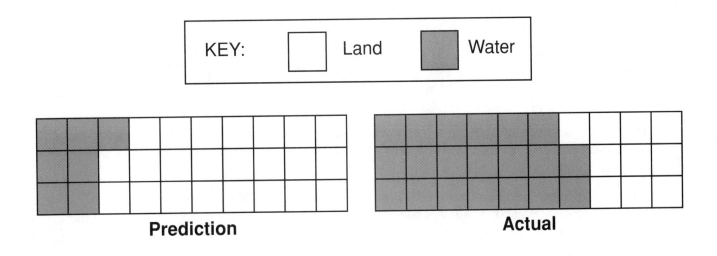

KEY: ☐ Land ▨ Water

Prediction   **Actual**

"I have learned the earth is mostly water," Michael said.

For an extension, have students draw a second Earth's surface picture representing the correct ratio, along with a sentence or two about what they have learned.

Types of Rocks I

1. Display these four sets of words: shiny/dull; hard/soft; rough/smooth; big/little (pages 12-15).

2. Discuss the meaning of each word by showing examples of each and allowing students to feel and see examples (hard - a piece of wood; soft - stuffed toy; rough - sand paper; smooth - aluminum foil; shiny - mirror; dull - construction paper).

3. Explain that rocks may be classified by how they look and feel. Show a rock for each type of feel/look description above. Allow students to hold and observe these various rocks. (Use these rocks for a class rock collection.)

4. As a class, classify each rock next to a corresponding descriptive index card.

    (**Note:** If students notice that rocks can be classified into three or more categories, make an appropriate card for those rocks.)

Teacher's Extra Reading Strategy: *Rocks and Minerals* by Illa Pondendorf (see Bibliography), is an excellent resource for making abstract concepts related to rocks understandable. You may decide to delete chapters or pages, if you feel they are too complicated for your students. Discuss the text and pictures as the pages are being read. Refer back to the class rock collection for hands-on understanding. Have students make a special sound (snap of fingers, whistle, clap) when they hear a word they have been introduced to during previous rock activities or lessons.

Three Kinds of Soil

Plants grow differently in different types of soils. The three kinds of soils are sandy, clay, and loam. Sandy soil contains a large amount of sand, clay contains tiny bits of clay, and loam contains decaying plants called humus. Let students find out which one is best by completing an experiment.

Divide the class into teams of three. Give each group the following: bags of each type of soil; fast growing seeds (peas, beans, radishes); three disposable cups or empty, clean, half-pint milk cartons; three spoons.

Each team member chooses one of the soils, fills a cup with it, and plants a seed at least one inch deep. Team members label their cup with the type of soil in it. They place them in a well-lit area. Each day team members take turns watering their seeds and recording what is happening with them. (Use the soil sheet on page 50.) As seeds grow into plants, let the students decide which soils the seeds liked the best.

Soil Sleep

Review the fact that soil is important to plants because it has air in it that plants breathe. Creatures live in soil, too, because they also stay alive by breathing the air found in it. Explain that some creatures live underground all the time, while other creatures live underground only some of the time. Some creatures take very long naps (hibernate) during cold winter months. Discuss the meaning of hibernate underground. Display six or seven pictures of creatures that hibernate (e.g., raccoon, snake, frog, squirrel, bear, mole). Divide the class into teams of four. Give each team directions/questions to be answered about a specific creature. When completed, allow each team to share results. (**Note:** For this activity, you may want to invite an older grade level to help students read books, encyclopedias, or stories to help them find their answer.)

The Magic School Bus® Inside the Earth

By Joanna Cole

Summary

Here is an award-winning book that is truly a delight to read. The science information has been superbly blended with the story of Ms. Frizzle and her class's underground adventure. Equally enjoyable are the "side" reports that Ms. Frizzle's class have written about what they learned during their magical adventure!

The outline below is a suggested plan for using the various activities presented in this unit. You may adapt the ideas to meet specific needs in your classroom environment.

Sample Plan

Day I

- "Rock" Salt (#1, Page 23)
- Create Magic School Bus Graph (#2, Page 23)
- Read *The Magic School Bus® Inside the Earth*
- Types of Rocks II (page 31)
- Learn Rock Facts Chant (#1, Page 24)
- Homework: Ms. Frizzle (page 27)

Day II

- Share Day I homework and display on Bulletin Board
- Paper Pressure (page 35)
- Make Peanut Butter Pressure (page 52)
- Discover Weathering Effects (#2, page 24)
- "Play" Time! (page 41)
- Chalk Art (page 60)

Day III

- Share and display Day II homework
- Cave Talk (page 35)
- Bake Cave Cookies (page 61)
- Cave Creatures (#4, page 25)
- Write On! (page 41)
- Homework: Cave Diorama (page 63)

Day IV

- Share and display Day III homework
- Three Types of Volcanoes (#5, page 25)
- Magma/Lava Language (page 36)
- Bake Volcano Cookies (page 62)
- Build a Volcano (#1, page 26)
- Excuse Me, Are You Sleeping? (page 57)
- Pumice Necklace (page 60)

Day V

- Beach Scene (#3, page 24)
- Sandy Situations (page 39)
- Make Sand-Cast Handprints (#2, page 26)
- Sandy Weigh-Ins (page 45)
- Desert Sands (#6, page 25)
- Sand Paper Spelling (page 43)
- Homework: Sand Dried Flowers (page 59)

Day VI

- Present prepared play from Day II
- Review/Reteach using several of the "More Rocky Ideas" (page 70) or additional Across the Curriculum Activities (page 40)
- Evaluation and Culminating Activities (page 64)

Overview of Activities

SETTING THE STAGE

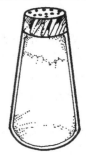

1. Show the class a clear container of salt. But don't tell them what it is, rather share that these are very special white rocks! Pour a little pinch into each student's hand. Ask them to observe the special rocks carefully. Allow them to look more closely through a magnifying glass. How do the rocks look? Share that we use these important rocks everyday. Let them guess what the rocks are called. Ask them to taste the rocks and discover that they are grains of salt. (Salt grains are really tiny cubic rock crystals.)

2. Show the cover of *The Magic School Bus® Inside the Earth*. Read the title. Ask students if the bus can really be magic. Make a quick graph by handing out square sticky notes and having students draw a happy face for yes or a sad face for no. Students come up to the front and place their sticky notes onto chart paper. Discuss which has the most and which has the least. Read the story straight through. (**Note:** For today's reading, do not read the "side paper reports" done by the students. These can be used later.) Talk about the story and the pre-graphed responses. Now read "A Word With the Author and the Artist." Re-evaluate the bus graph. Can a real bus go to the center of the earth? Ask students if they want to change their answers.

3. Weathering (wind, water, and ice) turns large mountains of rock into "rocks." Place rocks about the size of your fist in a sturdy bag. Hit the rocks with a hammer five times. Have students observe the rocks now. How have they changed? What made them change? (The hammer symbolizes the "weathering effect.") Record the changes. Place rocks back into bag. Repeat by hitting the rocks five more times, observe, and record again. Continue until the rocks become very fine sand/soil. Discuss.

Overview of Activities *(cont.)*

ENJOYING THE BOOK

1. Create a chant of facts learned from the story. Using the example given, model the idea in a large group. If students are able, divide into teams and allow them to create additional lines to the chant. When the chant is completed, repeat it together. Display chant and re-read occasionally.

Soil, Soil, Soil

dirt, on top, below.

Rocks, Rocks, Rocks,

hard, layers, white.

Fossils, Fossils, Fossils,

dinosaurs, leaves, soft.

Caves, Caves, Caves

dark, wet, stalagmites!

Rocks, Rocks, Rocks,

heat, pressure changed.

Rocks, Rocks, Rocks,

lava, melted, cooled.

Rocks, Rocks, Rocks,

hot, hotter, hottest.

Rocks, Rocks, Rocks,

chalk, blocks, and our parking lot!

2. Display a fan (wind), water (rain), and ice cubes (ice). Share that rocks change because of the wind, rain, and ice. Fill three boxes with sand. Put the fan close to one box and turn on. Have students describe what they see happening! Repeat with water and ice. Discuss how weathering affects rocks. Ask students to think of any place they have seen weather affecting rocks. Share answers. Go out and see if you can find any weathering effects such as potholes, or cracks in the sidewalk.

3. Draw a beach scene of the seashore and water on a piece of butcher paper. Display. Have students brainstorm as many items as they can think of that are made from or contain sand. List on the beach scene with a marker.

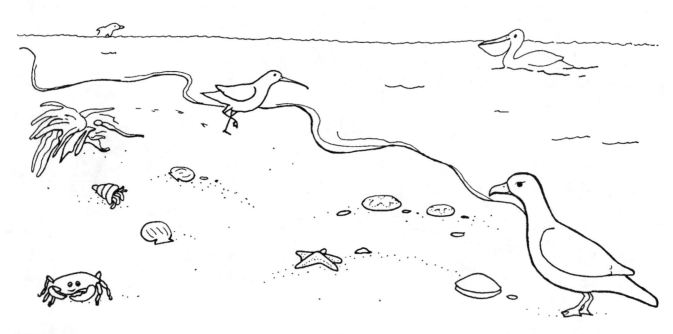

24

Overview of Activities *(cont.)*

4. Since caves are usually underground, they do not get light from the sun. Have students read (or you read to them) about animals and insects that live in dark caves. Refer back to *The Magic School Bus® Inside the Earth* pages which discuss caves and cave formations, as well. Make a class mural of the inside of a cave on a large piece of butcher paper. Each student draws and colors a separate picture of a cave dweller and pastes it to the mural. Display the mural in a hallway with the title "Creature From _____ (class name) Cave."

5. Discuss the three types of volcanoes. Use visual aids, pages 28 to 30.

Composite Volcano

Cinder Cone Volcano

Shield Volcano

(semi-rounded)

(smooth and rounded)

(peaked)

Using modeling clay, allow students to create their own volcanoes, choosing the shape they feel is most interesting to them. Group the finished volcanoes. Compare to see which volcano was made the greatest number of times, the least number of times, and if any were made an equal number of times.

6. Deserts are full of sand! When the wind blows, the sands in the desert begin to move. (Sand from African deserts has been found in China!) Discuss sand dunes and show pictures of them. Divide the class into teams of four students each. Place a pile of fine sand on a piece of newspaper in front of each group. Hand out a straw to each team member. Ask them to blow on the sand for a few minutes; share designs. (**Note:** Caution students not to blow too hard, or they will get sand in their eyes.) Change members of the teams and try again. Did the patterns come out the same or different? Why?

Overview of Activities *(cont.)*

EXTENDING THE BOOK

1. Build a volcano. Give each child a marble-sized ball of clay and a cone-shaped cup. Have the children put their names on the cups. Place the ball of clay inside the point of the cup. Mix plaster of Paris, about 8 lbs. for a class of 30, a little bit at a time, to the consistency of thick pancake batter. Put the mix into the cups and let set for 24 hours. Then give the children their volcanoes and several sheets of newspaper. Have them peel away the cup and remove the clay ball. They should have a volcano with a crater. Stand the volcano upright on the spread-out newspaper. Prepare the volcano for an eruption. Place about one teaspoon of baking soda into the "crater" which has been lined with plastic wrap. Mix red & yellow food coloring with ½ teaspoon of white vinegar in a separate cup. Pour the vinegar slowly into the baking soda. Observe what happens!

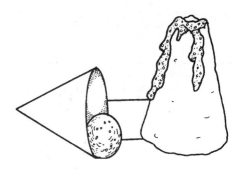

2. Sand-Cast Handprint. Create a special sand memory that your students will cherish. Ask parents to come in and help. To complete one sand-cast handprint, you will need:

    > medium-size gift box; water;
    > aluminum foil; sand; plaster of Paris;
    > spoon

    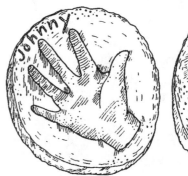

    A. Line the bottom and sides of the box with foil.

    B. Fill box half-way with sand. Add enough water sprinkled on top to make sand moist.

    C. Smooth sand evenly. Press hand down into sand to make deep impression.

    D. Mix plaster of Paris with water to form a thick creamy texture. Spoon into the impression. Add additional plaster to form a circle over the impression. Let dry completely by placing out in the direct sun. It may take two full days of sunshine before it is dry.

    E. Lift out cast and brush off the sand. Student names can be written on paperweights with a permanent marker. Students may use paperweights on their desks, or take home for a special gift!

    F. Have students write a special "Sand Poem" to go along with their handprint gift!

Name _____

Ms. Frizzle

Ms. Frizzle Loves to wear Crazy outfits to "show" what she is teaching.

Make a new outfit for Ms. Frizzle!

What is she teaching?

_____

Cinder Cone Volcano

Composite Volcano

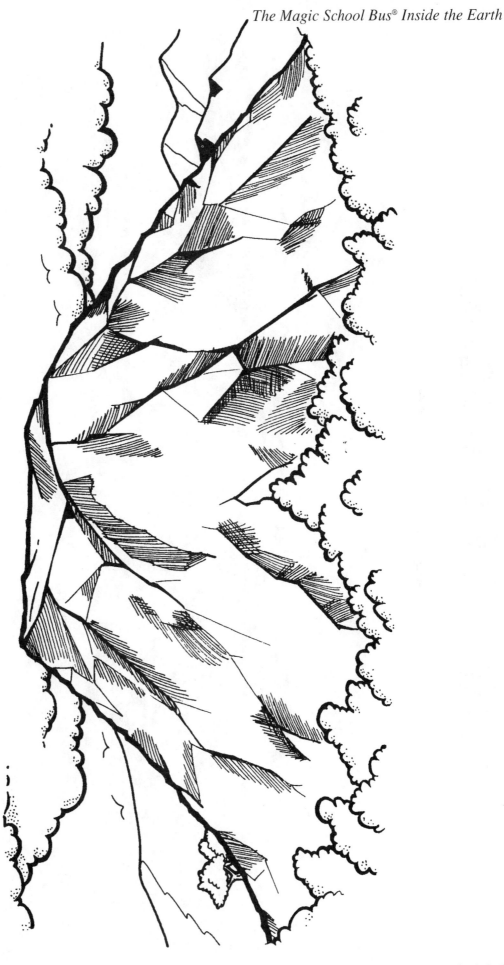

Shield Volcano

Types of Rocks II

Use the same format as Types of Rocks I (page 20), add three descriptive words (pages 32-34): texture = rough/smooth; hardness = hard/soft; luster = shiny/dull. Add an additional activity by placing the rocks in a bag and having students feel the rocks to see if they can classify them correctly without using their eyes!

Rocks are actually classified into three types:

Name	Characteristics	Cause/Effect	Usually Found
Igneous (granite, basalt, obsidian, pumice, quartz)	glossy, crystalline, coarse-grained	created when molten lava cools	where volcanoes have existed
Metamorphic (slate. schists, migmatite, marble, eclogite)	hard, crystals may appear, layers may develop	created when sedimentary or igneous rocks undergo a change due to pressure or heat within the earth	deep in the earth where pressure and heat can affect the rocks
Sedimentary (chalk, coal, sandstone, shale, limestone, dolomite)	contains fossils, soft, layered	created when layers of sediment (mud, sand, gravel, and minerals) settle to the bottom of the ocean and over thousands of years are pressed together	where oceans or bodies of water once existed or still exist

Use the word cards on pages 33 and 34. Discuss word meanings and show examples of the three types of rock. Compare the rocks using descriptive cards. Create a compare and contrast circle graph for the three classified rock types.

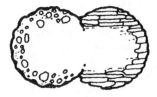  

Rock Description Cards

Rock Description Cards *(cont.)*

Rock Description Cards *(cont.)*

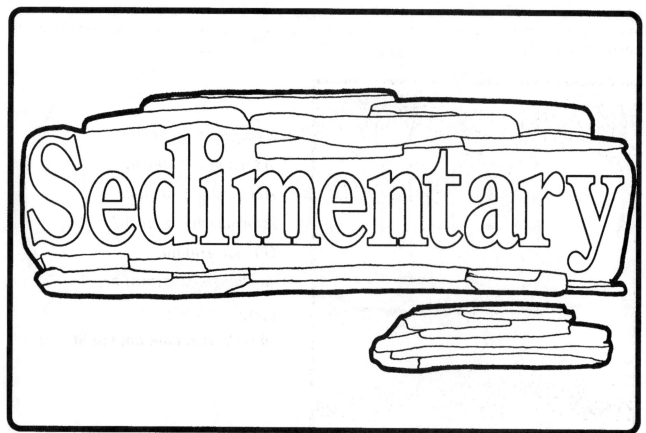

34

Mountains, Valleys, and Caves

Paper Pressure

Hand out pieces of brown construction paper. Ask students to bow the paper up at the ends (Figure 1) while you model with your paper. Ask what it looks like (a valley). Ask how the side walls of rock move up (pressure). Have students flatten their paper. This time ask them to create a mountain by bowing paper in the opposite direction (Figure 2). What caused the mountain to rise in the middle (pressure)? Explain that this is what happens to large pieces of rock. When the pressure moves the big pieces, little pieces break off and make smaller rocks. Paint with thick tempera; allow to dry; then bend to see cracking and flaking. Have students review what they have learned by working with partners and creating mountains and valleys with their paper.

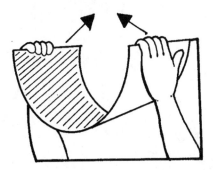 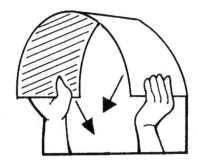

Cave Talk

Teach students how to remember where the "stalagmites" and "stalactites" are located in a cave. Draw a picture as shown below on the chalkboard. Write the word to describe each rock formation in the correct area. Using colored chalk, put a circle around the "g" and "c" in each word. As a class, repeat the poem below. Students then draw their own cave scene, label their rock formations, and write out the cave poem.

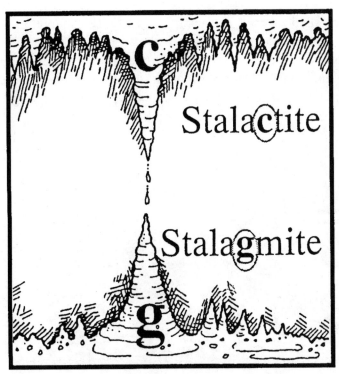

Stalagmite, stalactite
Which one is which?
Here's a way to make
remembering a cinch!
G is for ground,
so stalagmite it must be,
C is for ceiling
so stalactite, look up, you'll see!

Magma/Lava Language

What is the difference between magma and lava? Write the two words on the board. Pose the question and list student responses. Hand out worksheet (page 38). Display the provided volcano chart (page 37).

Using the chart, explain that heat from the layers in the mantle and inner core makes the rocks so hot they melt! Pressure forces the hot rock up toward the earth's crust. The hot, liquid rock comes out of the crust wherever it finds a hole.

Volcanos are big holes. The reason they turn into mountains is because the hot, liquid rock shoots out of the hole and lands near the hole. It cools off and becomes hard rock again. When this process happens over and over again, the cooled, hard rock forms layers that become thicker and thicker. From the outside of the volcano we can't see the layers, but if we look inside a volcano we can. (Point to the volcano chart, page 37.)
Have students label their worksheets using page 37. You may wish to discuss and label together.

Volcano (väl **kā** no) n. 1 . a vent in the earth's crust through which molten rock and ashes are ejected 2. a cone-shaped mountain built up by molten rock and ashes.

Crater

Lava

Side vent

Crust

Magma chamber

Students should notice that the hot, melted rock is called magma, but when it spurts out the name changes to lava. Ask why. The answer is: When the hot, melted rock is inside the earth it picks up minerals and gases. These two items change the way the rock is made. When it reaches the surface, the hot, melted rock is not the same anymore. It is actually a different kind of rock; therefore, two different names! Display the labeled volcanoes on a bulletin board, or in the hallway, along with sentence strips written by each student, explaining the difference between the two kinds of rock.

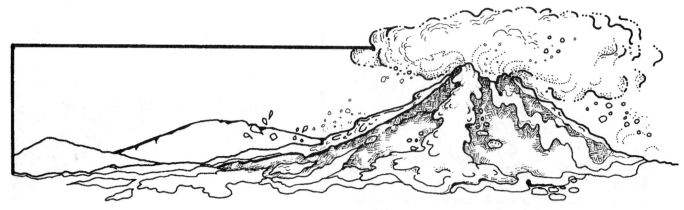

Volcano

Volcano (väl **kā** no) n. 1. a vent in the earth's crust through which molten rock and ashes are ejected 2. a cone-shaped mountain built up by molten rock and ashes.

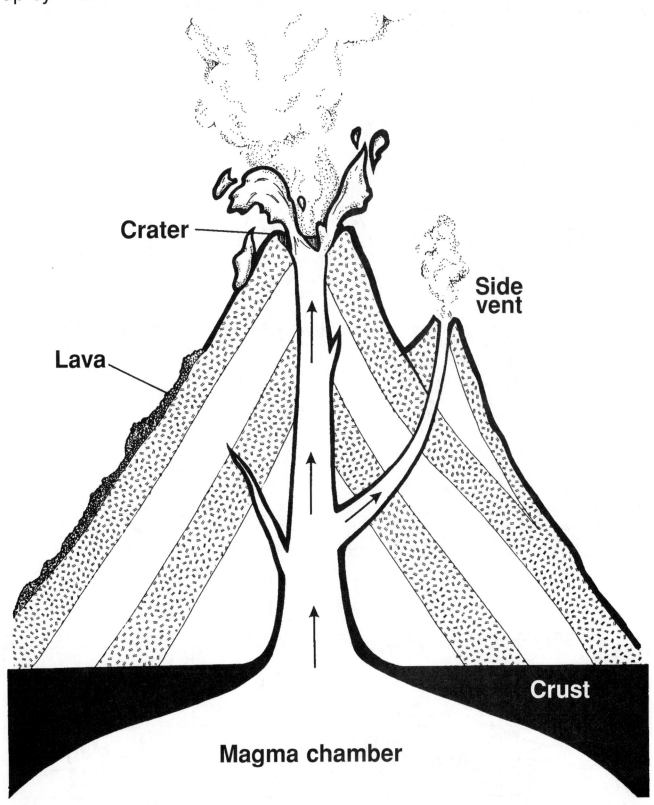

Crater

Side vent

Lava

Crust

Magma chamber

NAME_____

Volcano Diagram

Label the volcano.

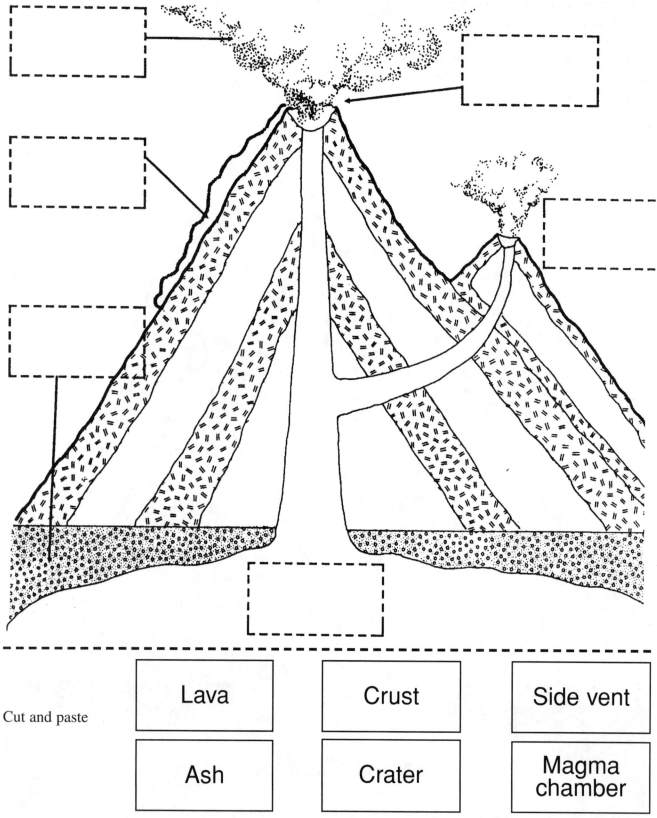

Cut and paste

Lava	Crust	Side vent
Ash	Crater	Magma chamber

Sandy Situations

Sand is actually small pieces of rock. Sandstone starts off as beach or river sand. After millions of years, minerals grow between the tiny grains and "cement" them together to form solid rock. Since minerals come in lots of colors, the layers of sandstone (like in the Grand Canyon) come in lots of colors, too. Show pictures, if available.

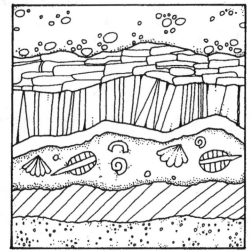

Make a layered sandstone picture by following the directions below. You will need:

pencils	water
white construction paper	plastic spoons
sand	paper towels
paper cups	liquid white glue
liquid food coloring	small paintbrushes

Note: Pre-dye sand a few days before this activity by filling paper cups half-full with sand. Add water to the cup until sand is completely covered. Add drops of one color of food coloring per cup (the more drops, the more vibrant the color). Stir the sand, water, and food dye using the spoon. Let set for 20 minutes. Pour off as much liquid as possible without pouring out the sand. Spread drained sand on paper towels and let dry completely. For variety, you can try different color combinations.

A. Draw lines with pencil across construction paper.

B. Squirt a small amount of glue in one area. Spread around with paintbrush.

C. Sprinkle one color of dyed sand in that area. Shake off excess.

D. Repeat with other sands to create colorful layers. Set aside to dry. Display sand paintings around one or more large pictures of the Grand Canyon, Painted Desert, or other multi-colored sandstone scene.

Rocky Writing Activities

Note to teacher: To help students reach their maximum writing potential enlist the help of volunteers or aides during these activities.

What An Adventure!

Write a story about your own adventure through the earth. What did you do, see, smell, hear, feel? Don't forget illustrations! (**Note:** For extra fun, use the no-spaceship on page 17 as a front cover and cut no-spaceship shapes out of writing paper for the story writing process!)

Clay Creatures

Clay is a form of rock. Have students create a Clay Creature using various colors of clay, and then write stories about their creatures! Encourage students to include a beginning, middle, ending, and title for their story. Have students share their stories and describe their Clay Creatures with a writing partner. Display stories/ creatures in the library for all to read and share!

Mood Rocks

Students create a "mood rock" by finding a flat, round stone and painting a happy face on one side and a sad face on the other. When the rocks are dry, students place their feeling mood rocks on the corner of their desks and write about a time that they remember feeling happy, as well as a time they remember feeling sad. Leave mood rocks on desks so students can show how they are feeling daily.

Rocky Writing Activities *(cont.)*

"Play" Time!

Create a class play of *The Magic School Bus®* adventure. Students will need to make up their own lines, create scenery, and write invitations for others to come and watch. Provide a little extra time throughout the day for play practice. When students feel they are ready, perform, perform, perform!

Write On!

Pre-determine the words that you feel are important for your students' spelling/language enrichment (page 79). List the words on the board or on brown construction paper rocks. Explain meanings in context of today's story or by looking up in a dictionary. Practice spelling the words in teams using "clay" pebbles or "disappearing word" rocks (salt). Then have students use the words in simple sentences to check for definition mastery.

"Report" To the Listening Center!

Copy the students' reports from *The Magic School Bus®* onto lined notebook paper, or have students write their own one-page reports. Make enough copies for a listening center. Have students share in reading the text and ringing a bell to signify turning the pages into a tape recorder. When completed, place tape and booklets in the listening area for all to enjoy!

Language Arts Activities

The Crow and the Pitcher

An Aesop's Fable

Promote the love of classical literature, while fostering critical thinking!

Place a clear pitcher half-full of blue colored (food coloring) water. Ask students to share how they think they can get the blue water to reach the top without adding water. List ideas on a large sheet of butcher paper.

Read or tell the Aesop's fable, *The Crow and the Pitcher*. In this fable a thirsty crow finds a pitcher with water in it. Try as she might, she could not reach the water in the pitcher. She felt as if she might die of thirst. Finally she figured out a way to get the water. She started dropping pebbles into the pitcher. With each pebble the water rose nearer the top until as last it reached the brim, and the crow was able to quench her thirst.

Experiment

Discuss why adding the pebbles made the water rise. Divide class into teams of two and give each team a small paper cup half-full of colored water. As a team, each group predicts how many marbles they will need to add to make the water reach the top of their cup. Hand out the quoted number to each group. Taking turns, the team members add one marble at a time to their cups. Lead a group discussion about their results. Some may need more marbles; some may need less. For an extension try the same experiment with various sizes of cups.

Language Arts Activities *(cont.)*

Important Rock Big Book

Create an Important Rock Big Book (adapted from *The Important Book* by Margaret Wise Brown). Cut out large rock-shaped pieces of paper. Write the sentence "A rock is important because . . ." at the bottom of the pages or on a paper strip which your students can glue to the page. Have students complete the sentences in groups or individually. Using brown or tan construction paper, create a rock-shaped Big Book cover. Collect the pages and bind with yarn or metal rings. Read and display.

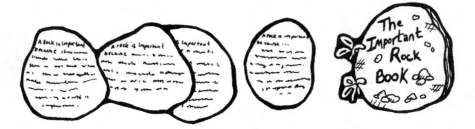

Sandpaper Spelling

If students are learning the alphabet letters (or idea can be adapted to reading series words), cut the letter shapes out of sandpaper.* Allow students to make letter rubbings with crayons using the sandpaper shapes covered by plain white paper. Students can combine letters to form words and build sentences.

* For easy cutting, trace the letter pattern backwards on the backside of the sheet of sandpaper; trace around letter pattern with pen and cut out.

"Rock"-A-Bye Baby

Brainstorm various sayings containing the word rock candy, hard as a rock, rock climbing, rock hound, rock around the clock, rock-a-bye baby, rock and roll). Write stories or poems using these sayings.

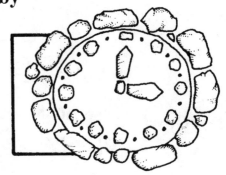

Language Arts Activities *(cont.)*

Story Starter Titles

Reproduce the rocks with story starter titles (see below). Glue onto brown paper. Cut out. Pass out one "rock" to each student. Using the title as their "starter," they write a story. Share and display finished writings. Students can also write a poem, song, or play!

Students can brainstorm their own titles, too. A blank rock is provided for students to write them on.

Math Activities

Sandy Weigh-Ins

Weigh various objects in the classroom using spoonfuls of sand. On a balancing scale, place a small object on one side of the scale. Using a tablespoon measure, have students scoop up sand and count how many spoonfuls are needed to equal the weight of the small object. Predict number of scoops before measuring begins. Record answer on chart paper. Continue with various objects of different sizes and shapes. Display completed chart with names of objects, predictions, and results.

Earthly Comparisons

Practice using the terms "greater than" and "less than" by comparing the various thicknesses of the earth. Students may have difficulty understanding the actual numbers (they are quite large!), so it may be more comprehensible to use an alternate, equally-portioned method (see chart below). Using colored link blocks, unifix cubes, or other types of interlocking cubes, allow students to create the layers. When layers have been assembled, ask various questions (e.g., Which layer is greater than the size of the earth's core?)

Layers	Actual Depth	Proportional Lengths
Topsoil	50 feet	Cover the top of the cube with masking tape (which represents the earth's crust)
Crust	44 miles	1 cube
Mantle	1,800 miles	41 cubes
Outer Core	1,430 miles	33 cubes
Inner Core	750 miles (to center)	17 cubes

Math Activities *(cont.)*

Soil Math Background

Provide students with a copy of pages 47 and 48. Give each a copy of the math manipulative (see below) to color and cut out. Ask a student to come up and help you demonstrate. Make up a problem similar to this: "I saw three worms in the soil...," (child puts three worms onto the soil background), "...and then I saw two more worms...," (child adds two more worms, "...so how many worms are in the soil now?"). Student then counts and gives you the response. Now have the same student tell you a soil math problem and you place the manipulative onto the background. Once you feel that all understand the process, allow students to tell each other their own soil story problems. (**Note:** This activity can easily be adapted to more difficult story problems. Another suggestion involves adding an extension in which students also write out the story problem they are completing.)

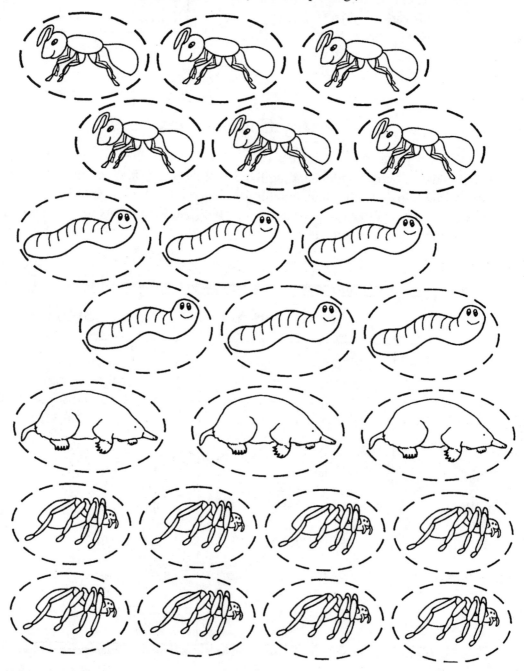

Deep, Deep, Underground

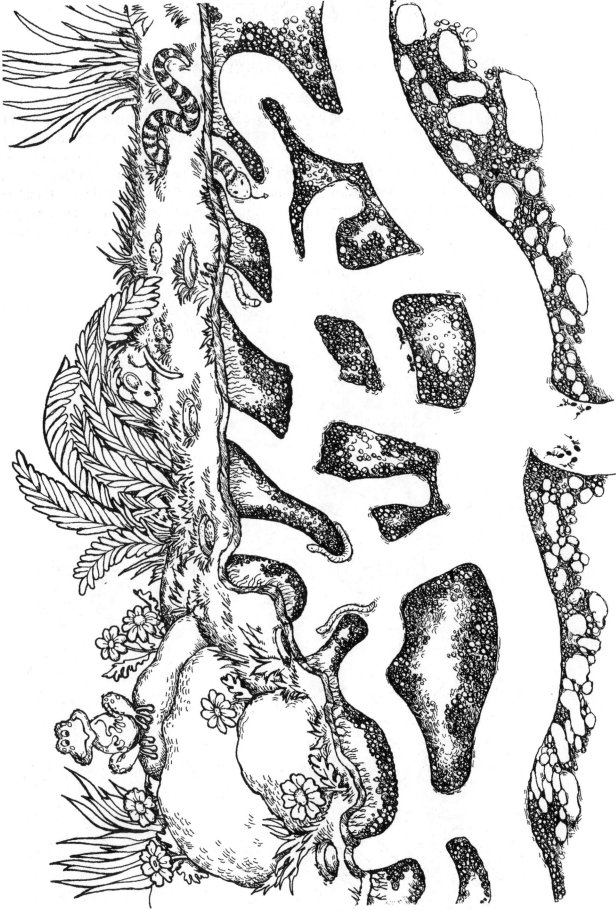

Deep, Deep, Underground *(cont.)*

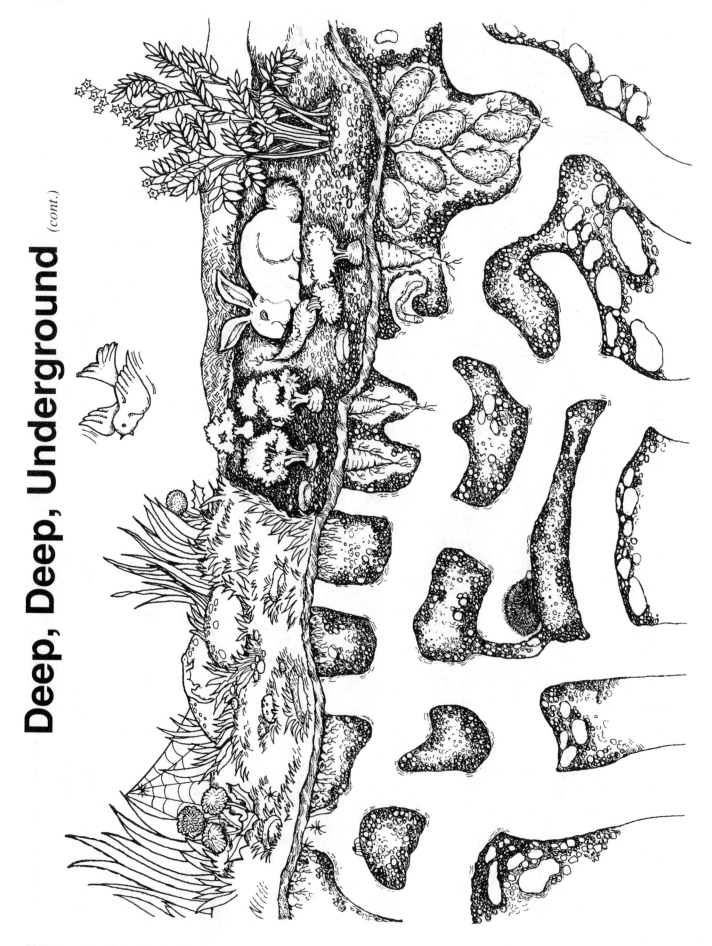

Math/Science Activities

Six Soil Speculations

Soil can be classified into three basic groups. Sandy soil contains a large amount of sand. Clay soil contains tiny clay particles. Loam soil has a large amount of humus (decaying plants). Each looks and feels different. Plants will grow differently in each of these soils. Which one is best? Complete and experiment to find out! Provide bags of each type of soil and one type of fast-growing seeds (peas, beans, radishes). Divide the class into teams of three.

A. Provide each team with three disposable cups or emptied, clean half-pint milk cartons, three spoons, and seeds. Set up three working areas, along with the three varieties of soil. Each team member chooses one type of soil and fills his/her cup. Plant seeds at least one inch below the top soil; label the cups with the soil type. Team members take turns each day to water their seeds and record what is happening to their plants on their soil sheet (page 50).

B. Next follow the format for A above, but add a math twist! Provide each team with three more cups. Besides the first three different soil types, challenge the teams to create their own mixtures for the remaining three cups ($\frac{1}{2}$ sandy soil; $\frac{1}{2}$ loam; $\frac{1}{2}$ sandy soil; etc.) Be certain that they label these cups properly so they know what mixtures they have used. For recording purposes, they will need a second soil sheet to note the progress of their three additional cups.

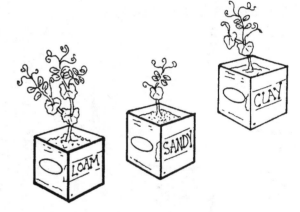

C. After a few days of care, the students should see growth in one or more cups. Let them use rulers to measure the growth. After a full week, have students decide which is the best soil for growing plants and record their answer on their soil sheet.

My Pet Rock

Ask students to go outside and find a rock no larger that their fist. This is their new pet rock. They are going to learn about their new friend. Have students use the worksheet on page 51 to complete the activity. (**Note:** To complete the experiment and learn about their new friend, the class will need to use rulers, scales and weights, pennies, nails, vinegar, eye droppers, containers of water, and paper or cloth towels. If available, have soft rock samples for comparing. A few types could be pumice, chalk, limestone. Examples of volcanic rocks would also be helpful.) Collect all worksheets when completed and make a "Class Pet Rock Book" for all to view, along with creating a display of the rock-rific pets!

Math/Science Activities *(cont.)*

Which Soil Is Best?

Team _____

Which soil is best for your seeds? Circle one.

SANDY SOIL   CLAY SOIL   LOAM SOIL

What type of seed did you plant in your three soils? _____

What is the day you planted your seeds? _____

Observe your seeds every day. Water seeds every other day. After one week, measure the growth. Using your ruler to get the correct length, draw what you see in the correct pot below.

Sandy soil

Clay soil

Loam soil

Which soil was the best to grow your seeds? _____

Why?_____

_____

_____

_____

_____

Math/Science Activities *(cont.)*

Pet Rock Experiment

Draw a picture of your rock here:

Where did you find your rock?

_____

Check the correct boxes.

My rock is:

☐ SHINY   ☐ DULL   ☐ HARD   ☐ SOFT   ☐ ROUGH

☐ SPARKLY   ☐ NOT SPARKLY   ☐ BIG   ☐ LITTLE   ☐ SMOOTH

Now conduct your experiment. Predict what you think the answers will be and write them down in the first row. After the experiment, write down the results. Compare.

	**LENGTH** Measure with a ruler.	**WEIGHT** Measure with a scale.	**HARDNESS** Which will scratch your rock?* 	**ACID**  Does your Rock Bubble when vinegar is dropped on it?**	**FLOATS** Does your rock float or sink?***
PREDICTION					
RESULTS					

Hardness Numbers

* Hardness scale: Fingernail can scratch rock 2   A soft rock

Penny can scratch rock 3

Nail can scratch rock 4   A hard rock

** If there are bubbles appearing on your rock, it has lime (or calcium carbonate) in it. This mineral is found in limestone and marble.

*** Rocks that float usually have come out of a volcano. Was the area where you live ever a volcano?

Science Activities

Peanut Butter Pressure

Students should now understand that the earth is made up of layers. These layers of rocks are affected by pressures. Depending on the type of rock and amount of pressure, different things can happen to the rock. Create a wonderful kinesthetic experience to insure the understanding of this principle.

For a class of 26 students you will need:

> 26 slices of dark-colored bread
> (pumpernickel or rye work well)
> 26 slices wheat bread (containing whole
> grains for "little rocks" making it even more
> realistic)
> 26 slices white bread
> Very large jar or container of peanut butter
> 13 butter or plastic knives
> 13 large plastic cups (to hold peanut butter)
> 26 paper plates

Remove the crusts from the bread.

Re-look at the diagram of the earth's layers (see page 16). Emphasize that most of the changes happen in the earth's crust layer. The crust is also made of separate layers. Explain that they are going to create their own crust layers and see what happens when they apply pressure to the crust!

A. Divide the class into teams of two. They will need to sit close to each other to share the peanut butter and knife. Give each student a paper plate and each team a knife and cup of peanut butter. Ask the teams to show they are ready to be good listeners, so that they will build their crust layers correctly.

B. Give the following directions:

1. Place white bread on your plate.

2. Spread peanut butter on top of the white bread.

3. Put the whole wheat bread on top of the peanut butter.

4. Spread more peanut butter on top of the wheat bread.

5. Put the dark bread, the top layer, on top of the peanut butter.

You've now made the earth's crust!

Science Activities *(cont.)*

Peanut Butter Pressure *(cont.)*

C. Have students push their own palms together, or push their partner's palms together. What they are feeling is called pressure. They are now going to push and cause pressure on their own crust layers.

D. Push sides in, causing the middle of the crust to come up. What did you make? (A mountain.) What has happened to the layers? (They are curving like a rainbow.) Discuss why. Let your crust go flat again.

E. Push the sides of your crust up. What did it make? (A valley.) What happened to the layers? (They look like a smile.) Discuss the reasons. Let your crust go flat again.

F. Take turns and ask your partner to make a mountain and a valley from his/her crust. (Allow a few minutes for teams to complete this task while you move around the room and observe.)

G. So far we have made our crust into a mountain and a valley. Can you think of anything else that can happen to the crust? Allow for responses. (Responses should include that rocks sometimes just "stick out" of the ground.) Explain that they are now going to make their crust have an earthquake experience. Ask students to cut their sandwich in half and hold one sandwich half in each hand, trying to keep the two cut halves together. When you give the signal (the word "Earthquake!") they are to move one half of their sandwich up. This will be like the pressure in the earth pushing up a section of the crust. Give the signal. Have students look closely at what happens to the layers. (They are not even across anymore! For example, the bottom white layer may now be aligned with the other half's middle wheat layer.) Discuss what this might mean to someone who wants to study the earth's crust.

H. Allow teams to give each other the signal and have their crust "experience" a few earthquakes.

I. Conduct an overall discussion about what they have learned as they eat their earth's crust! (Be sure to hand out a drink, too. The earth's crust can be a bit dry!)

Extension: Watch a film on how the earth is affected by pressure (for example, "Pressure and Change Beneath the Earth's Surface," Our Changing Earth filmstrip series from American School Publishers). Stop film/ VCR at appropriate times to discuss main points.

Science Activities *(cont.)*

A Soily Experience

Emphasize that soil is important to us. Plants will not live unless they can get air, water, and food from the soil around them. Show an inexpensive, small, potted plant. Ask how the plant gets the things it needs through the roots. Have students observe as you uproot the plant. Shake the soil off the roots and allow students to observe closely through a magnifying glass. Explain that the root has little hairs called "root hairs." The food, air, and water go through the hairs and into the plant. Explain that they are going to investigate different soils to see if root hairs would be happy there! Divide the class into teams of four. Provide each team with a brown bag, spoon, glass container with lid, newspaper, paper cup, and magnifying glass. Have each group pick out a location card from a container (pre-written by teacher telling students where they will have to go outside to collect their soil; e.g., near cafeteria, by swings). Teams collect their soil in the brown bag. When they return to the classroom each group follows the steps below:

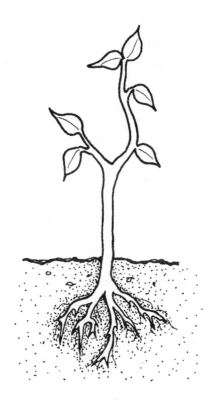

A. Pour soil onto newspaper. Feel soil. Observe soil through magnifying glass.

B. Fill your jar ¹/₃ full of soil. Pour water into jar using the paper cup. Pour slowly! What is happening to the soil? Fill the jar ²/₃ full of water.

C. Put your jar lid on tight! Take turns and shake your jar. Set it down on the table. Watch what happens!

D. While soils in jars are settling, observe the other groups' jars (place location card next to jar). How are the soils alike or different?

E. As a total group, with the teacher leading discussion, observe and discuss each settled-soil jar. (**Note:** More layers means there are more air holes in soil; large amount of decayed leaves equals good source of food for a plant.) Decide which area(s) around school would be the best for growing plants.

Science Activities *(cont.)*

Our Egg-ceptional Earth

Provide each student, or every other student, with a hard boiled egg. Display picture of the earth's layers (see page 16). Review the boy's travels in his no-spaceship. Discuss the name of each layer of the earth (topsoil/crust, mantle, core). Ask how their egg is like the earth. Under adult supervision, cut each egg in half (right through the shell!). Students can now visually see the similarities (yolk = core; egg white = mantle; shell = crust/topsoil). Together, discuss how they are alike. To finish up the activity, let the students taste their mantle and core, but no eating the crust!

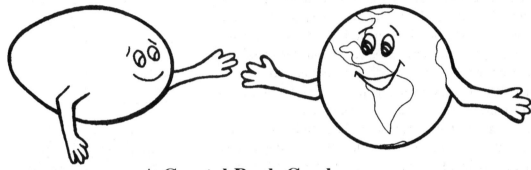

A Crystal Rock Garden

Divide students into teams of four or five. Provide each team with a small metal tray and one piece of charcoal (briquettes) each. Students place their special rocks in the tray and come to a designated mixing area to mix the following solution under adult supervision: ½ cup water, ½ cup salt, ½ cup liquid blueing, 1 cup ammonia. They then pour the mixture over their charcoal pieces and squirt the charcoal with red, green and/or blue food dye. Place the trays in a corner of the room (please do not disturb!), and wait one day. Hooray, crystals!

Science Activities *(cont.)*

An Ant Farm

Divide the class into four groups. Ask an adult volunteer to help in each group. (Discuss how to put the ant farms together with the volunteers prior to activity time.) Provide each group with the following materials:

large-sized wide mouth jar	rich soil
water	big rubber band
bread or graham crackers crumbs	baby food jar
30 ants (from the same colony)	2 large sheets black construction paper
eye dropper	tablespoon
sand	sugar
cheese cloth	masking tape
large spoon	white chalk

Have each group put together their ant farms following the procedure below:

1. Place the baby food jar upside down in the bottom of the large jar.

2. Mix together an equal amount of sand and soil. Using the spoon, put soil around the sides and top of the baby food jar. (Be sure to leave the sand and soil loose to form air pockets so the ants can breathe!)

3. Mix two tablespoons of water with one tablespoon of sugar. Fill eye dropper and squirt drops into the soil. Add a handful of graham cracker or bread crumbs.

4. Put the ants in the large jar. Cover the mouth of the large jar with cheesecloth. Secure it with a rubber band, just under the rim.

5. Cover the outside and top of the ant farm with the black construction paper, using tape to secure. (This will make the ants think they are underground, where there is no light.) Write the group's name with chalk on the black construction paper.

6. Keep the ant farms quiet by placing in a safe corner of the room.

7. Each day for one school week, remove top piece of construction paper and feed the ants sugar water and graham cracker or bread crumbs by dropping through the cheesecloth. Re-cover with construction paper. In five days, remove all of the black paper and see the amazing tunnels the ants have created!

8. Take the ant farms outside and let the ants go back to their own soil. Be sure to say thank you to the ants for helping you learn!

56

Social Studies Activities

**Excuse Me,
Are You Sleeping?**

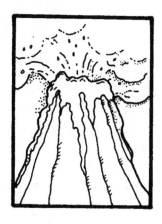

Dormant

A dormant volcano is one that
is not spurting out magma. It is
said to be "sleeping."

Active

An active volcano is one that is
spurting out magma, causing lava
and ash to flow down its sides!

Using various resources, discover where dormant versus active volcanoes exist in the world. Read books, watch films or look at videos about the eruption of famous volcanoes (for example, *Volcano*, a video of Patricia Lauber's 1987 Newbery Honor Book about Mount St. Helens available from American School Publishers). Discuss what they have seen after each book/movie presentation, encouraging descriptive word usage.

Chart active and dormant volcanoes on a classroom globe. Use two colors of star stickers and attach onto globe at the locations. Have students create a key to the Volcano Globe. Place globe and key in school library for all to view!

Social Studies Activities *(cont.)*

Soil Helps Us

Show the class a potted plant. Explain that soil helps people. Show real objects that have been created due to the use of soil. Some examples may be clothes made from cotton, fresh vegetables or fruits, a door or other wooden items, a picture or model of a house, furniture. Ask how soil was responsible for these objects. Discuss. Ask how our world would be if we could not grow things in the soil. (An important point to make is that we would die because we get our oxygen from the plants that grow in the soil!) Divide the class into teams of three. Provide each team with three large pieces of white butcher paper. On each piece of paper students are to draw soil at the bottom of the paper, with a large plant or tree growing out of the soil. Each tree needs to be labeled "Food"; "Clothes"; "Furniture." Provide magazines. Students find appropriate pictures to add to their plants/trees as the leaves. Display all groups of trees (along with a short explanation on sentence strips of why soil is important to us) in the hallway for all to see!

The Grand Canyon

Show a picture of the Grand Canyon. This is one of the best examples of layers of sandstone. Sandstone is a type of sedimentary rock. It is very soft. Count the layers of sandstone rock in the pictures of the Grand Canyon. Explain that the older sandstone is at the bottom of the canyon, while the newest sandstone is at the top. Let students hypothesize why this is true. Discuss. If possible, finish discussion with a film or VCR tape about the Grand Canyon!

Gold Dust!

Contact a local hobby shop. They often have a group of people who enjoy the hobby of panning for gold. This is done by finding rivers and streams with gold deposits nearby. Panners sift the sand in the bottom of the waters to find gold flakes. Invite a panner to come to your classroom. Ask the guest speaker if he/she can help you set up a mock panning experience for students to enjoy, and see how it feels to strike gold!

Art Activities

Sand Dried Flowers

Have your parents or an older brother or sister help you with this project!

Gather flowers from a field, or get a bunch from a local flower shop. Keep them looking pretty for a long time by drying them in sand.

You will need:

- a cardboard box
- sand
- scissors
- freshly picked flowers
- drinking straws
- pipe cleaner
- green construction paper
- white glue

1. Fill the box half-full of sand. Cut away most of the stem from each flower (leave about 1 inch).

2. Push the stem of each flower into the sand in the box.

3. Carefully sprinkle more sand over the flowers until they are all covered up. Place the box in a dry place (maybe a closet, or in the attic). Let the flowers stay there for at least two weeks!

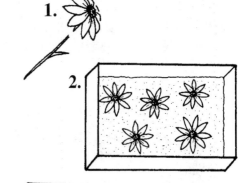

4. When flowers are dry, carefully remove them from the sand in the box. Put the stem of a flower into a drinking straw. Wrap a pipe cleaner around the stem and straw to hold them together.

5. Cut out leaves from the green construction paper and attach to straw with some glue.

6. Bring in your beautiful bouquet of dried flowers for all your class to see!

Art and Music Activities

Pumice Necklace

Pumice is the most porous stone. It is actually hardened foam that bubbled out of a volcano. It is the only stone that floats. (Pumice stone can be purchased at most grocery stores in a rectangular shape.) Cut stones into one inch blocks. Make enough blocks so each student will receive three one-inch stones. Hand out stones and a string to make necklace. Discuss what pumice is. Challenge students to create their own holes through the middle of the stones. When they have accomplished this, string the stones. For homework ask them to wear their stone necklace in the bathtub and sink down into the water to watch it float!

Chalk Art

Chalk is a rock! It is a form of limestone, often found in layers of pressurized rock. Create a piece of art using a rock. Provide chalk and black construction paper. Students use their "soft rocks" to create a picture. Display. For a fun alternative have students draw a picture of a friend's face with another kind of soft rock; a pencil! Display the finished pictures on a bulletin board with the title "Stone-Faced."

Soil Song

Sing the soil song (written below) with your class to the tune of "Mary Had a Little Lamb." After students understand the pattern and the meaning, let them write a soil song of their own. This can be done to the same or a different tune, as well as in a large or small group setting. If done in small groups, allow time for all groups to share their newly-written songs. (Songs can be recorded and placed in a listening center area.)

Soil Song

Soil helps us every day, every day, every day,

Soil helps us every day,

To work, and rest, and play!

Soil has special needs, special needs, special needs

Soil has special needs,

Water, air, and food!

Cooking and Physical Education Activities

Rock Candy

Utensils: measuring cup

large saucepan or pot

spoon

baby food jars

pencils

4" length of soft cord (one per student)

Ingredients: 8 cups of water

16 cups of sugar

A. To prepare the jars, have each student tie the string around the center of pencil, allowing a two-inch length to hang down from the pencil. Balance the pencil on the rim of a baby food jar; set aside.

B. Heat 8 cups of water mixed with 16 cups of sugar over medium heat.

C. When sugar has dissolved, continue to add sugar until no more dissolves.

D. Remove pot from stove and let cool until just warm.

E. Have students place their prepared jars on a table. Pour sugar mixtures into the jars around string and pencil. Set jars aside. Within a few hours crystals will begin to form. Leave overnight.

F. Pull candy string out of the liquid in the jar and enjoy!

Note: If you pour the remaining sugar liquid from all the jars back into the pot, reboil, and proceed with step E again, the string of rock candy will grow even larger.

Cave Cookies

Make "Cave Cookies" by wrapping walnut-sized pieces of chilled sugar cookie dough around chocolate kisses. Place on ungreased cookie sheet, pressing down slightly to create a flat bottom. Bake according to cookie dough recipe. Remove and cool completely. When students bite into their cookies, they will see the inside of a dark cave!

Cooking and Physical Education Activities *(cont.)*

Volcano Cookies

Using a chilled, stiff sugar cookie dough, shape a walnut-sized piece into a volcano and place on cookie sheet. Make a small depression in the top with your pinkie. Spoon a small amount of red jelly or preserves in the depression. Bake according to the recipe, allowing cookies to brown slightly. Cool completely and enjoy! (**Note:** While cookies are baking, have students predict which of the three types of volcanoes their cookies will appear to be!)

Earthly Physical Education

Using chalk on a large blacktop area, or lime (used for making the lines on a baseball diamond) in a large, grassy field, create a proportionally-sized cross-section of the layers of the earth. (See diagram on page 16 for help in determining proper proportions.) Label each layer with large cards. Designate students or parent helpers to hold them up. Ask students to hop to the earth's core, run backwards to the earth's crust, skip through the earth's mantle, and so on. For variety let them guess how many hops or seconds it will take to get from one layer to another.

Beware, Quicksand!

Jack Be Nimble, Jack Be Quick, Jack Jump Over the Quicksand, Quick! Instead of the typical long jump event seen in most track and field events (designed to create only a few winners), let everyone be a winner by drawing a line in the sand (or dirt, if no sand is nearby) and another line six inches away. Have everyone jump over the quicksand, quick! After everyone has jumped over the quicksand, redraw the second line another six inches farther and start again. Continue adding six inches until you decide to end the game.

Sand Between My Toes

If your class has access to a sandbox area, go out and "experience" the sand. Feel it, describe it, smell it. Play, build, and write in it. Squiggle toes, pat cakes, and build roads in it.

Homework Activities

Cool Tool!

Create a new digging tool from things you can find around your house. Give it a special name. What is it made of? How was it put together? What are its special uses?

Rock Hunt

Students are to find 12 rocks from around their house and yard. Encourage them to have an adult help them in their hunt. Together they are to classify and label the rocks found and bring them in the next day for a display in the library. (**Note:** Egg cartons are perfect for creating rock displays.)

Mystery Hole

Ask students to get together with their parents and dig a hole in the backyard! What will they use the hole for? Have them draw a picture of their family using the hole. Write a sentence or two explaining why their family chose the project/ activity for the hole.

Cave Diorama

Provide each student with an empty shoe box. Students are to create a cave scene inside their box. Have each share their diorama with the class and then put them on display in the school library!

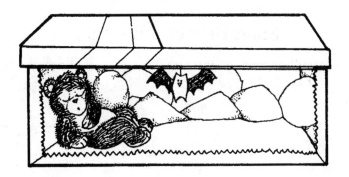

Evaluation & Culminating Activities

On your evaluation and culminating activity day, allow adequate time to complete the following experiences (times are approximate):

> **Career Choices** - 30 to 60 minutes
>
> **Verbal Discussion** - 15 minutes
>
> **Evaluation** - 30 minutes
>
> **Achievement Awards** - 10 minutes
>
> **Culminating Activity** - will vary depending on activity chosen

Career Choices

There are two types of careers associated with the study of the earth and the materials that make it.

Geologist - studies rocks and soils to find minerals, oil, and precious metals

Paleontologist - studies fossils (the remains of plants and animals in soft rocks)

There are many activities that can increase students' awareness of careers in geology and paleontology. Choose some of the activities on the following pages to complete with your class.

There are several other careers associated with the earth, including ecologist, archaeologist, miner, gemologist, seismologist, and oceanographer. For extension activities, have students do further research on some of these earth-related careers and share the information with the class.

Evaluation & Culminating Activities *(cont.)*

I Can Be a Geologist by Paul P. Sipiera is an excellent and simple resource to be read to your students. The illustrations show the jobs and responsibilities of a geologist. After reading this book, complete one or more of the following activities:

Role-Playing: Make Geologist Play Boxes by collecting multiples of the following items: rock hammer, rocks, hard hat, microscope, fossil, clip board, pencil, pen, burlap sack, ruler, land maps. Encourage students to act out what a geologist does when working. If working with older students, list and discuss vocabulary words (page 79) on the board to broaden their verbal dialogues.

Vocabulary Development: The geologist uses some special tools. As a class discuss each tool and its use. Teach the correct spelling and pronunciation of each word.

Guest Speaker: Invite a real geologist to the class. If possible, request that the geologist bring some of the more unusual apparatus used during the work day. After the guest speaker leaves, write thank you letters including illustrations of the geologist at work.

Math: Geologists have to be able to inspect rocks carefully. Provide rocks to teams of students and allow them to weigh, measure, and categorize the rocks by various weights and/or sizes. Display rocks in a sequenced order form smallest to largest or lightest to heaviest.

Science: A paleontologist studies rocks that contain fossils. If your class has not made fossils, do so now.

Create a Fossil!

Provide each student with the following supplies:

1½ pints (720 mL) milk carton cleaned and dried (cut top section off)

1 bar modeling clay

A choice of "fossil" items (shell, leaves, bones, etc.)

A. Have students press their modeling clay into the bottom of their cartons and smooth out the top of the clay.

B. Press the chosen "fossil item" firmly into the clay; remove.

C. Prepare a mixture of plaster of Paris and pour a layer of plaster over each student's impression until it is completely covered. Set aside to dry.

D. Tear the milk carton away from the clay and plaster. Separate the plaster from the clay. You now have a fossil!

Note: This type of fossil is called a "positive fossil." To create a "negative fossil" grease the top of the positive fossil with petroleum jelly and place in a second prepared milk carton. Pour a second layer of the plaster of Paris mixture over the positive fossil until it is completely covered. Set aside to dry. Remove carton and separate the fossil. Now you have two different kinds of fossils!

Evaluation & Culminating Activities *(cont.)*

Guest Speaker: Invite a paleontologist to come and share fossils that have been preserved in layers of sandstone. Incorporate what students have learned from previous lessons about the different types of rocks in the earth. Remind them that fossils can be found in sedimentary rock. Ask what kind of creatures they think fossils used to be. Use the fossils to discuss how, over millions of years, the bones were covered over with soil and pressed together. With time, the bones dissolved and all that was left was the imprint or fossil.

After the visit, write thank you letters using the stationery on page 78 or your own, sharing what has been learned!

Art: Geologist I-Spy Glasses. Geologists and paleontologists have to be able to locate rocks and fossils in some unusual places. Follow the directions to make special I-Spy glasses. Take completed glasses outside and have students look through them to see if they can spy different sizes, shapes, and types of rocks (and maybe even a fossil)!

To make one pair of I-Spy Glasses, you will need:

> 2 toilet paper rolls
>
> tempera paint
>
> glue
>
> hole puncher
>
> string or yarn

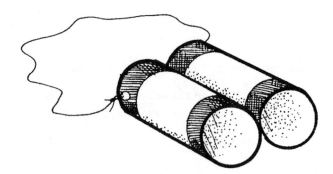

1. Paint paper rolls desired color. Let dry.

2. Glue tubes together to form "binoculars."

3. Punch a hole on the outside edge of each tube.

4. Attach an 18" (46 cm) piece of string to both holes to form a strap to wear around the neck. Enjoy an I-Spy Rock and Soil Hunt!

Evaluation & Culminating Activities *(cont.)*

Discussion

This is an excellent time to review what the students have learned during this thematic unit. Encourage students to share their feelings or facts about the following:

favorite new rock fact	favorite new soil fact
layers of the earth	something new never known before
different types of rocks	different types of soils
favorite homework activity	favorite class activity
how mountains are formed	three types of volcanoes
how to protect our earth	how to stop soil erosion

The teacher can simply ask questions about these or other related topics, or write them on cards and have students choose one and share the answer. Be certain that everyone who chooses to participate gets a chance to share. After sharing, move on to evaluation time.

Evaluation Time

Evaluation can be done in a variety of ways. Here are a few suggestions:

1. Written Evaluation—Teacher chosen questions

2. Written Evaluation—Student-generated questions

3. Verbal Evaluation—Teacher asks a series of pre-determined questions one-on-one with student and records mastery/non-mastery of skills and concepts.

4. Web Evaluation—Before beginning the rocks and soil unit, post a web drawn on chart paper. In the center write Rocks and Soil with black marker. Have students brainstorm all the facts they know about this topic; accept and write down all responses using a black marking pen. Put web away until testing day. Pull web from its hiding place and post. Students or the teacher reads facts on the web. Students tell teacher if fact is correct (leaves as is), incorrect (cross out), or is partially incorrect (make necessary changes suggested by students) using a red marker. Compare and evaluate what the students have learned during this unit.

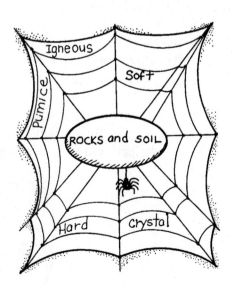

After evaluation has been completed, move on to achievement awards.

Evaluation & Culminating Activities *(cont.)*

Achievement Awards

Achievement awards are fun to give out because they show that everyone in the class is a winner!

Here are a few suggestions for awards.

1. Use the awards (page 77) and hand one out to each student.

2. Create Rock Hound rock awards by cutting brown construction paper to resemble rocks. Spread a thin layer of glue over paper rock and sprinkle gold or silver glitter. Add blue crepe paper ribbons and attach to each Rock Hound with a straight pin.

3. Have students create their own awards. Collect and write in students' names, making sure that the award was made by a fellow student. Pass out to students. After awards are presented, move on to culminating activity.

Earth Awareness

There are a variety of activities that can be used for the culminating activity. It should be noted that the activities listed below were chosen considering the sequencing of this thematic unit. Students should now have a true understanding of how and what the earth really is. Your students are the "next generation." It is our duty to make them aware that we must take care of our earth. (If you wish to extend your study of care of the earth, Teacher Created Resources Thematic Units, TCM 272 *Our Environment* and TCM 286 *Ecology* are excellent resources.) The activities below are designed with this important concept in mind.

1. **Recycling Picnic.** Plan a special picnic where all food is brought in containers that can be recycled. Share with the class that most people go to a picnic and just throw their trash in the garbage, or worse, on the ground! Their picnic is going to be special because they are going to recycle their food containers. On a large piece of butcher paper (shaped like a picnic basket, if you'd like) have students brainstorm all the kinds of containers they can bring that can be recycled (plastic, aluminum, foam). Send home a note to parents explaining the uniqueness of this recycling picnic. After students have enjoyed their picnic, have three large bags labeled Plastic; Aluminum; Foam, available for students to separate their garbage. Explain that you, or a special parent helper, will be delivering the recyclable containers to a recycling center after school.

Evaluation & Culminating Activities *(cont.)*

Earth Awareness *(cont.)*

2. **Recycling Rendezvous.** Plan a field trip to one or two types of recycling centers. Before going, start collecting recyclable containers from around the school. (For example, have you ever thought how many milk cartons are used in your lunch room by the whole school in one week?!) After the field trip, discuss what the students saw and learned at each recycling center.

3. **Junk Mail Junkies.** Discuss the meaning of what junk mail is a week before the culminating experience. Send home a note to student's parents asking that their child be allowed to save all the mail for one week that is considered "junk." These might include flyers, coupon inserts, envelopes, free newspapers. On the culminating day, have students bring all of their junk mail to class. Provide a large (and, yes, it will need to be large!) piece of butcher paper for students to paste or glue on all of their junk mail to form a collage. Add the title "What a Waste! " along with a brief explanation about the project. Place the collage and explanation in the hall for all to see, and join in the fight to cut down on paper garbage. For an added extension, place a recycling collection box by the collage for everyone to start throwing in their old or junk paper products. Bi-monthly take the paper to a recycling center. If the center gives cash for the paper, save it for a special end-of-the year Earth Day party!

4. **Design Bags.** Most plastic bags are non-biodegradable and add to the earth's pollution. We use paper bags that come from trees. We usually only use them once and throw them away. Use fabric to create bags that can be used over and over again. Sew or glue bags together. Decorate them. If you make them lunch-sized, students can bring them to school each day.

More Rocky Ideas!

- **Math: Underground Creature Counting Book.** Using heavy tagboard or lightweight cardboard, provide each student with eleven 4½" x 12" sheets (9" x 12" cut in half). On the cover write "My Creature Counting Book." Students color remaining pages to look like underground soil. Provide counters such as beans or noodles. On each page, students use a black crayon to write the appropriate number and glue on the corresponding amount of "creatures." For example:

  1 – one lima bean (they can leave plain, or add legs); 2 – two black beans; 3 – three crackers and so on until 10. Punch holes in left-hand side of finished pages and lace up with yarn or string. Use the counting books during math review or free choice time.

- **Art: Marble Painting.** Cover area with newspaper. Give each student a large piece of white construction paper. Place bright colors of tempera paint in shallow container. Place a few marbles in each container of paint. Students choose a marble covered with paint and lay it on their white paper.

  Picking up the edges, they roll the marbles around their paper. Return marbles to proper container, repeat with two or three other colors. Set aside marble art to dry. Display.

- **Poetry:** Read the poem entitled "Rocks" by Florence Parry Heide in *Sing a Song of Popcorn.* Have students create their own "earthy" poems.

More Rocky Ideas! *(cont.)*

- **Social Studies: Globe Watching.** Look carefully at a globe. Have students choose five spots on the globe and figure out where they would come out if they dug a hole through the earth at those locations. Have students draw pictures of the earth and label the enter and exit points of their adventures through the earth! Display.

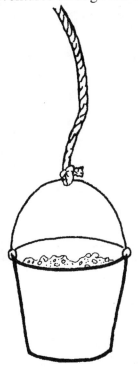

- **Story Extension:** Review the beginning of *How to Dig a Hole to the Other Side of the World.* Enlist the help of a strong person, and a shovel. Take the class outside and dig six feet deep. (Pre-approve the area first!) Stop at each foot interval and record student observations at each level. At the six-foot mark, see if clay or gravel has been reached. Discuss why, or why not, clay or gravel was found. For an extension place the soil in a bucket attached to a rope and have students take turns pulling up the bucket to examine its contents.

- **Story Writing: Rock Town Cartoons!**

Watch *Flintstone* cartoons on a VCR tape. Students will begin to notice that everything is made from rocks, even the town name, "Bedrock." Divide class into four writing teams and have each team create a new Rock Town cartoon. Encourage detailed illustrations. Have teams present their cartoons to each other or to a different grade/class.

Bulletin Board

Rock Hounds
UNITE!

Objective

This bulletin board has been designed to display students' work as they learn about rocks and soil. As students' work is placed on display, it can be used to review information and skills taught.

Materials

Colored butcher paper (blue for sky; brown or tan for soil); colored construction paper (for both Rocky the Rock Hound and the smiling rocks); scissors; tape or push pins; pre-made letters or markers (for lettering).

Construction

1. Reproduce patterns (page 74-76) onto appropriate paper and cut out.

2. Make lettering for title.

3. Place butcher paper pieces onto bulletin board for background. (Note: To add a "rough" effect, tear edge of brown paper instead of cutting to form soil area.)

4. Add Rocky the Rock Hound and two copies of the smiling rock pattern as shown above, or create your own design!

Bulletin Board *(cont.)*

Introduction of Bulletin Board

Explain the definition of a rock hound. Share that *How to Dig a Hole to the Other Side of the World* is about a boy who loves rocks and is a rock hound! He will be going on an exciting adventure. Read the title. Ask what the boy is doing. Why is he dressed in funny clothes? What is he using? Let's read and find out! This story can be read straight through or by stopping and discussing concepts on various pages.

Optional Uses

1. Reduce the size of the rocks patterns to approximately 4" x 6". Reproduce onto colored construction paper. Write a question pertaining to the rocks and soil information, or other skill being learned. Staple or pin to bulletin board near the top edge of rocks pattern. Place the correct answer underneath the smiling rock pattern and allow the bulletin board to be used as an interactive experience. (Students read the questions, think about the answers, then check for correct answers under the rocks!)

2. Use the bulletin board to display "good work" samples. Instead of the suggested title, replace with:

Work Worth Inspecting!

Display work on top of brown construction paper rocks.

Bulletin Board *(cont.)*

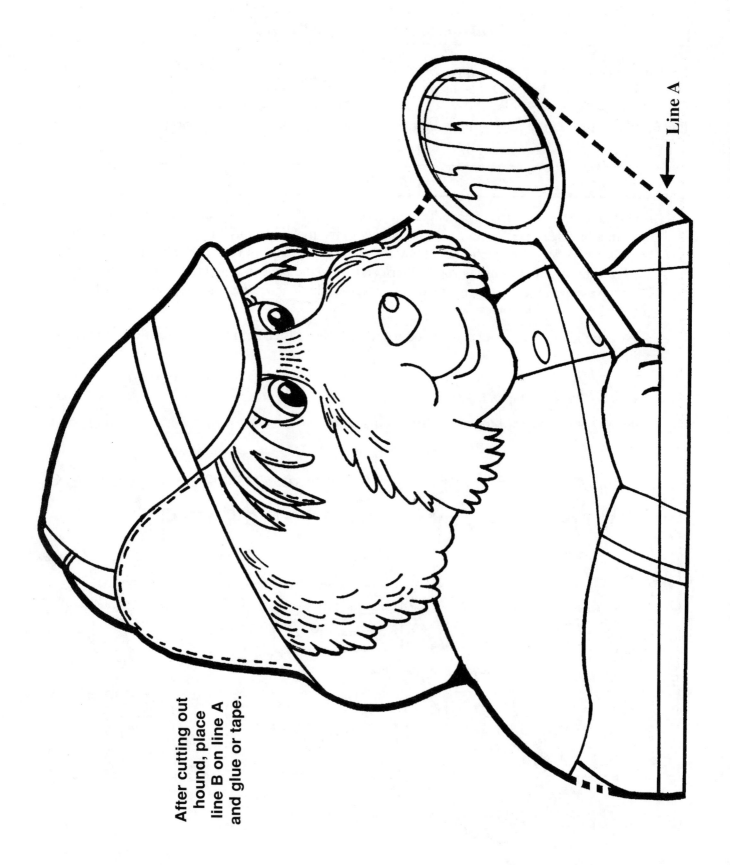

Line A

After cutting out hound, place line B on line A and glue or tape.

Bulletin Board *(cont.)*

Line B

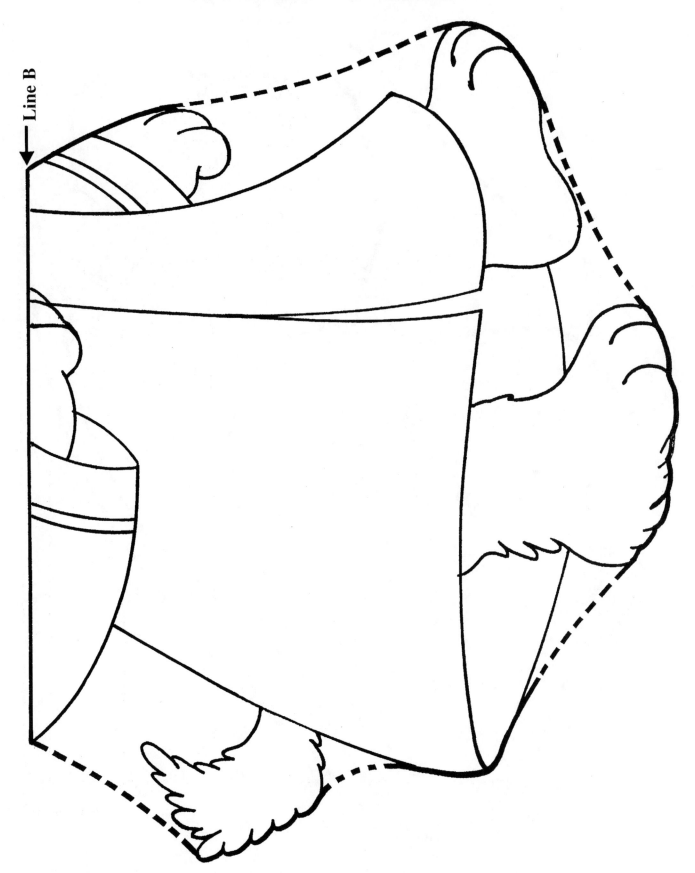

Bulletin Board *(cont.)*

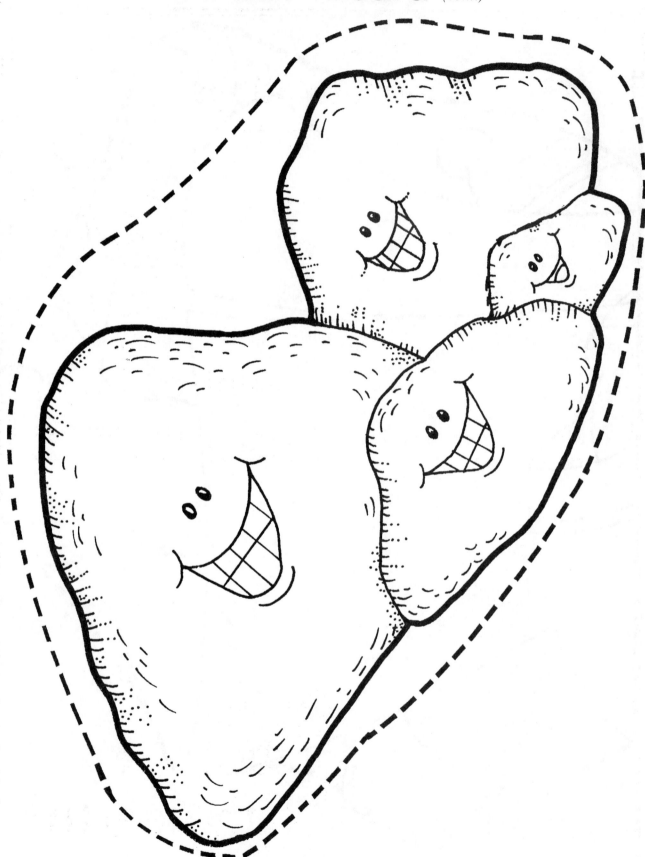

Awards

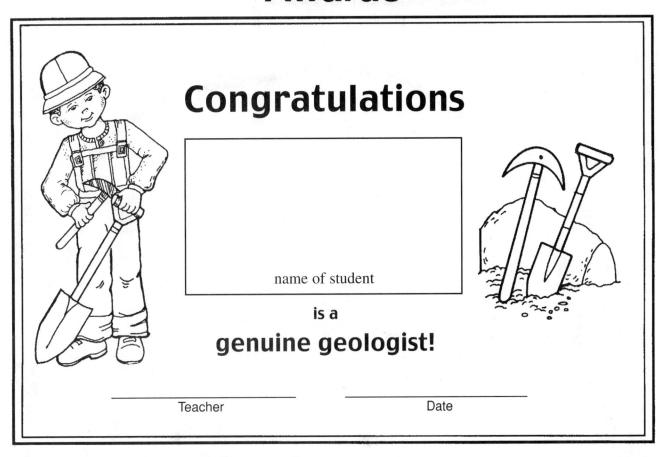

Congratulations

name of student

is a

genuine geologist!

_____   _____
Teacher   Date

Student's Name

cares
about
the earth!

Stationery

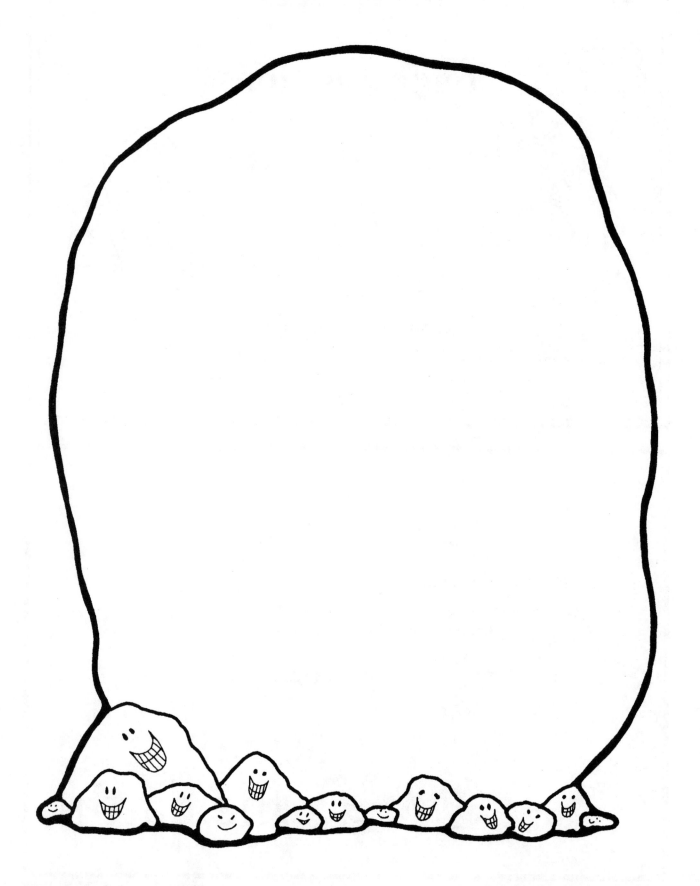

Rocks and Soil Vocabulary list

Easy Words . . .

rock	stone	soil	pebble	boulder
mountain	clay	hard	soft	rough
smooth	shiny	dull	sand	earth
layers	water	air	wind	garbage

Harder Words . . .

topsoil	crust	mantle	outer core	plants
texture	luster	hardness	pressure	inner core
weathering	cave	quicksand	loam	volcano
pollution	protect	creatures	soil	minerals

And just a little bit harder words . . .

igneous	metamorphic	sedimentary	magma
stalagmite	continent	decay	oxygen
shield volcano	lava	geologist	paleontologist
canyon	glacier	petroleum	compass
ecology	erosion	gemstone	composite volcano
seismograph	microscope	stalactite	cinder cone volcano
fossil	vent		

Rocks and Soil Bibliography

Literature

Aesop's Fables. "The Pitcher and the Crow." (any version)

Baylor, Byrd. *Everybody Needs a Rock.* (Aladdin, 1987)

Baylor, Byrd. *If You Are a Hunter of Fossils.* (Aladdin, 1980)

Cearly, Beverly. *The Real Hole.* (Dell Publishing, 1960)

Cole, Joanna. *The Magic School Bus® Inside the Earth.* (Scholastic, 1988)

Cooney, Barbara. *Miss Rumphius.* (Puffin, 1982)

dePaola, Tomie. *The Quicksand Book.* (Holiday House, 1977)

Dunrea, Olivier. *Deep Down Underground.* (Macmillan, 1987)

Ehlert, Lois. *Planting a Rainbow.* (HBJ, 1988)

Hiscok, Brice. *The Big Rock.* (Macmillan, 1988)

McNulty, Faith. *How to Dig a Hole to the Other Side of the World.* (Harper & Row, 1979)

Peet, Bill. *The Wump World.* (Houghton Mifflin, 1970)

Peters, Lisa Westberg. *The Sun, the Wind, and the Rain.* (Henry Holt, 1988)

Ryder, Joanne. *Under Your Feet.* (Four Winds Press, 1990)

Schenk de Regniers, sel. by. *Sing a Song of Popcorn.* (Scholastic, 1987)

Steig, William. *Sylvester and the Magic Pebble.* (Juvenile, 1988)

Wiethron, Randall. *Rock Finds a Friend.* (Green Tiger Press, 1988)

Zion, Gene. *Harry, the Dirty Dog* (Harper Trophy, 1956)

Resource Books

Aliki. *Fossils Tell of Long Ago.* (Harper & Row, 1972)

Barken, Joanne. *Rocks, Rocks Big and Small.* (Silver Press, 1990)

Branley, Franklin. *Earthquakes: Let's Read and Find Out.* (Thomas Crowell, 1990)

Fiarotta, Phyllis. *Snips and Snails and Walnut Whales.* (Workman, 1975)

Gans, Roma. *Caves.* (Harper Trophy, 1977)

Gans, Roma. *Rock Collection* (Harper Trophy, 1984)

Hyler, Nelson. *The How and Why Wonder Book of Rocks and Minerals.* (Price, Stern, and Sloan, 1987)

Jargenson, Eric. *Manure, Meadows, and Milkshakes.* (The Trust for Hidden Villa, 1986)

Javna, John and the Earth Works Group. *50 Simple Things Kids Can Do To Save the Earth.* (Universal Press, 1990)

Pondendorf, Illa. *Rocks and Minerals.* (Childrens Press, 1990)

Pondendorf, Illa. *Volcanos.* (Childrens Press, 1983)

Raferty, Kim and Devin. *Kid's Gardening: A Kid's Guide to Messing Around in the Dirt.* (Klutz Press, 1989)

Rinkhoff, Barbara. *Guess What Rocks Do?* (Lothrop, 1975)

Rose, May and Tom. *TREEmendous Activities for Young Children.* (Idea Factory, 1987)

Russell, Helen Ross. *Ten Minute Field Trips.* (Ferguson, 1973)

Selsman, M. *A First Look at Rocks.* (Walker, 1984)

Sipiera, Paul. *I Can Be a Geologist.* (Childrens Press, 1986)

Srogi, Lee Ann. *Start Collecting Rocks and Minerals.* (Running Press, 1989)

Stille, Darlene. *Soil Erosion and Pollution.* (Childrens Press, 1990)

The Earthworks Group. *50 Simple Things You Can Do To Save the Earth.* (Earthworks Press, 1989)

Updergraff, Imelda and Robert. *Mountains and Valleys.* (Puffin, 1980)

Webb, Angela. *Sand.* (Watts, 1987)

Webb, Angela. *Soil.* (Watts, 1987)

Whitfield, Philip. *Why Do Volcanoes Erupt?* (Viking, 1990)

Wyler, Rose. *Science Fun with Mud and Dirt.* (Messner, 1987)

Audio-Visual

The Changing Earth. (filmstrip) Silver Burdett

Teacher Created Resources

"Created by Teachers for Teachers"

Quality Resource Books
language arts
social studies
math
science
technology
the arts

Decorative Products
2-sided decorations
3-D decorations
accent dazzlers
awards
badges
banners
bookmarks
border trim
bulletin boards
file folders
incentive charts
name plates
name tags
notepads
pocket folders
postcards
stickers

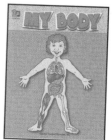

For more information, visit our Web site: www.teachercreated.com

ISBN 1-55734-265-2

50999

9 781557 342652

Teacher Created Resources

PRINTED IN U.S.A.

ISBN 1-55734-265-2

0 14467 00026

O5-KJB-920

LANDSCAPE GUIDE
FOR CANADIAN HOMES

Canada

CMHC SCHL

HOME TO CANADIANS